Q: Skills for Success
READING AND WRITING

3

Margot F. Gramer

Colin S. Ward

SERIES CONSULTANTS

Marguerite Ann Snow

Lawrence J. Zwier

VOCABULARY CONSULTANT

Cheryl Boyd Zimmerman

OXFORD

UNIVERSITY PRESS

OXFORD
UNIVERSITY PRESS

198 Madison Avenue
New York, NY 10016 USA

Great Clarendon Street, Oxford OX2 6DP UK

Oxford University Press is a department of the University of Oxford.
It furthers the University's objective of excellence in research, scholarship,
and education by publishing worldwide in

Oxford New York

Auckland Cape Town Dar es Salaam Hong Kong Karachi
Kuala Lumpur Madrid Melbourne Mexico City Nairobi
New Delhi Shanghai Taipei Toronto

With offices in

Argentina Austria Brazil Chile Czech Republic France Greece
Guatemala Hungary Italy Japan Poland Portugal Singapore
South Korea Switzerland Thailand Turkey Ukraine Vietnam

OXFORD and OXFORD ENGLISH are registered trademarks of
Oxford University Press in certain countries.

General Manager, American ELT: Laura Pearson
Publisher: Stephanie Karras
Associate Publishing Manager: Sharon Sargent
Managing Editors: Martin Coleman, Mary Whittemore
Associate Development Editors: Rebecca Mostov, Keyana Shaw
Director, ADP: Susan Sanguily
Executive Design Manager: Maj-Britt Hagsted
Associate Design Manager: Michael Steinhofer
Electronic Production Manager: Julie Armstrong
Production Artist: Elissa Santos
Cover Design: Molly Scanlon
Image Manager: Trisha Masterson
Image Editors: Liaht Pashayan
Production Coordinator: Elizabeth Matsumoto

ISBN: 978-0-19-475624-2 Reading Writing 3 Student Book Pack
ISBN: 978-0-19-475640-2 Reading Writing 3 Student Book
ISBN: 978-0-19-475621-1 Q Online Practice Student Access Code Card

Printed in China

This book is printed on paper from certified and well-managed sources.

10 9 8 7 6 5 4 3 2 1

ACKNOWLEDGMENTS

*The publisher would like to thank the following for their permission to reproduce
copyrighted material:* p. 54, "Practice Makes . . . Pain?" *Weekly Reader Senior*,
May 5, 2006. Special permission granted by Weekly Reader, published
and copyrighted by Weekly Reader Corporation. All rights reserved;
p. 117, "Happiness Is in the Shoes You Wear" from "Jesus Is a Brand of Jeans"
by Jean Kilbourne, *New Internationalist*, September 2006, Issue 393. Used with
kind permission of New Internationalist. Copyright New Internationalist.
www.newint.org; p. 121, "In Defense of Advertising" from *The Age of
Persuasion*, CBC Radio One, Terry O'Reilly and Mike Tennant. Used by
permission; p. 137, from "Fear Factor: Success and Risk in Extreme
Sports" by Brian Handwerk, *National Geographic News*, July 8, 2004,
http://news.nationalgeographic.com. Used by permission of National
Geographic; p. 143, "The Climb of My Life" from *The Climb of My Life:
Scaling Mountains with a Borrowed Heart* by Kelly Perkins. Copyright
© 2007. Used by permission of Rowman & Littlefield Publishers; p. 189, from
"Money makes you happy—if you spend it on others" by Carey Goldberg,
The Boston Globe, March 21, 2008. © 2008 *The Boston Globe*. All rights reserved;
p. 206, from "2b or not 2b?" *Txtng: The Gr8 Db8* by David Crystal, Oxford
University Press, 2008, as appeared in The Guardian, July 5, 2009, www.
guardian.co.uk. Used by permission of Oxford University Press.

*The publishers would like to thank the following for their kind permission to reproduce
photographs:* Cover Yukmin/Asia Images/Getty Images; Jupiter Images/
Workbook Stock/Getty Images; David Anderson/iStockphoto;
4x6/iStockphoto; Kuzma/iStockphoto; TrapdoorMedia/iStockphoto;
vi. Marcin Krygier/iStockphoto; xii. Rüstem GÜRLER/iStockphoto; p. 2 Chris
Ryan/OJO Images/Getty Images; p. 4 Blend Images/Alamy (office); p. 4 Kevin
Dodge/Corbis UK Ltd. (cafe); p. 6 The Image Bank/Getty Images; p. 7 Joseph C.
Justice Jr./iStockphoto; p. 12 Comstock Images/Getty Images; p. 24 Eric
Futran - Chefshots/FoodPix/Getty Images; p. 28 California California/Alamy;
p. 46 DIMITAR DILKOFF/AFP/Getty Images; p. 50 Glowimages/Getty Images
(blue car); p. 50 Gary Sims/Alamy (yellow car); p. 55 Eileen Langsley
Gymnastics/Alamy; p. 56 William Ju/Alamy; p. 59 Andrew Fox/Alamy;
p. 61 Oleksiy Maksymenko/Alamy; p. 66 Julian Ward/Flickr/Getty Images;
p. 70 Blend Images/Alamy; p. 71 Peter Cade/Stone/Getty Images; p. 76 Tony
Cordoza/Alamy; p. 77 Ethno Images, Inc./Alamy; 88 Sylvain Grandadam/age
fotostock; p. 90 fotoshoot/Alamy (changing tire); p. 90 imagewerks/Getty
Images (wheelchair); p. 90 Bart Geerligs/Getty Images (purse snatcher);
p. 90 Eddie Linssen/alamy (map); p. 92 Nathan King/Alamy; p. 94 Inspirestock
Inc./Alamy; p. 100 Corbis/Digital Stock/Oxford University Press;
p. 112 AP Photo/Nati Harnik; p. 114 dmac/Alamy (billboard); p. 114 Neil
Setchfield/Alamy (chicken); p. 114 Howard Davies/Alamy (climate change);
p. 114 Justin Kase z03z/Alamy (truck); p. 116 Image Source/Alamy;
p. 117 Reuters/Corbis UK Ltd.; p. 121 Bruce Laurance/Getty Images;
p. 132 Marcelo Hernadez/LatinContent/Getty Images; p. 134 Aurora Photos/
Alamy (skiing); p. 134 AFP/Getty Images (mountain climbing); p. 134 Image
Source/Oxford University Press (rock climbing); p. 134 Ace Stock Limited/
Alamy (motocross); p. 134 Peter Arnold, Inc./Alamy (rafting); p. 134 Nick
Chaldakov/Alamy (bungee); p. 134 Jiri Rezac/Alamy (steelworker);
p. 134 David R. Frazier Photolibrary, Inc./Alamy (logger); p. 134 Associated
Press/Press Association Images (roofer); p. 134 Mark Richardson/Oxford
University Press (farmer); p. 134 David Wells/Alamy (fisherman);
p. 134 Vladimirs Koskins/Shutterstock (painter); p. 137 Koji Aoki/
Aflo Foto Agency/Photolibrary Group; p. 144 M. Timothy O'Keefe/Alamy;
p. 154 Rafael Campillo/age fotostock; p. 156 SVLuma/Shutterstock (bicycle);
p. 156 Photodisc/Oxford University Press (carrots); p. 156 Doug Steley A/
Alamy (bag); p. 159 Foster and Partners; p. 165 frank'n'focus/Alamy;
p. 166 Tomas Rodriguez/Corbis UK Ltd.; p. 169 Libby Welch/Alamy;
p. 173 Patrick Batchelder/Alamy; p. 178 David Snyder/ZUMA Press;
p. 180 JKlingebiel/Shutterstock (sheep); p. 180 Photodisc/Oxford University
Press (bee); p. 180 Stephen Dorey/Oxford University Press (goat); p. 180
Martin Rugner/age fotostock (chicks); p. 180 Shutterstock (slikworms);
p. 180 GWImages/Shutterstock (stationary); p. 182 The Canadian Press/Press
Association Images; p. 183 Sheila Doherty/Heifer International (Beatrice);
p. 183 Darren K. Fisher/Shutterstock (cap); p. 190 Ilene MacDonald/Alamy;
p. 202 Brian Pieters/Masterfile; p. 204 Alex Mares-Manton/Asia Images RM/
Photolibrary Group; p. 206 MCNG Photography/Alamy; p. 207 Sutton-Hibbert/
Rex Features; p. 213 Andersen Ross/Blend Images/Corbis UK Ltd.

Illustrations by: p. 4 Bill Smith Group; p. 11 Stuart Bradford; p. 26 Barb Bastian;
p. 29 Karen Minot; p. 34 Karen Minot (all); p. 68 Bill Smith Group; p. 156 Bill
Smith Group; p. 204 Barb Bastian.

ACKNOWLEDGEMENTS

Authors

Margot F. Gramer holds an M.A. in TESOL from Teachers College, Columbia University. She has been involved in the field of ESL as a teacher, teacher-trainer, administrator, writer and editor. She has taught ESL for many years at both the college level and in business settings. She is the author or co-author of many ESL textbooks. She is currently an Instructor at the Language Immersion Program at Nassau Community College (LINCC) in Garden City, New York.

Colin S. Ward holds an M.A. in TESOL from the University of London. He has been teaching English for nearly ten years. His interests include the teaching of second-language writing and the role of technology in language learning. Colin is a U.S.-U.K. Fulbright scholar and the author of several ESL textbooks.

Series Consultants

Marguerite Ann Snow holds a Ph.D. in Applied Linguistics from UCLA. She is a professor in the Charter College of Education at California State University, Los Angeles where she teaches in the TESOL M.A. program. She has published in *TESOL Quarterly*, *Applied Linguistics*, and *The Modern Language Journal*. She has been a Fulbright scholar in Hong Kong and Cyprus. In 2006, she received the President's Distinguished Professor award at Cal State L.A. In addition to working closely with ESL and mainstream public school teachers in the United States, she has trained EFL teachers in Algeria, Argentina, Brazil, Egypt, Japan, Morocco, Pakistan, Spain, and Turkey. Her main interests are integrated content and language instruction, English for Academic Purposes, and standards for English teaching and learning.

Lawrence J. Zwier holds an M.A. in TESL from the University of Minnesota. He is currently the Associate Director for Curriculum Development at the English Language Center at Michigan State University in East Lansing. He has taught ESL/EFL in the United States, Saudi Arabia, Malaysia, Japan, and Singapore. He is a frequent TESOL conference presenter and has published many ESL/EFL books in the areas of test-preparation, vocabulary, and reading, including *Inside Reading 2* for Oxford University Press.

Vocabulary Consultant

Cheryl Boyd Zimmerman is associate professor of TESOL at California State University, Fullerton. She specializes in second-language vocabulary acquisition, an area in which she is widely published. She teaches graduate courses on second-language acquisition, culture, vocabulary, and the fundamentals of TESOL and is a frequent invited speaker on topics related to vocabulary teaching and learning. She is the author of *Word Knowledge: A Vocabulary Teacher's Handbook*, and Series Director of *Inside Reading*, both published by Oxford University Press.

REVIEWERS

We would like to acknowledge the advice of teachers from all over the world who participated in online reviews, focus groups, and editorial reviews. We relied heavily on teacher input throughout the extensive development process of the Q series, and many of the features in the series came directly from feedback we gathered from teachers in the classroom. We are grateful to all who helped.

UNITED STATES Marcarena Aguilar, North Harris College, TX; Deborah Anholt, Lewis and Clark College, OR; Robert Anzelde, Oakton Community College, IL; Arlys Arnold, University of Minnesota, MN; Marcia Arthur, Renton Technical College, WA; Anne Bachmann, Clackamas Community College, OR; Ron Balsamo, Santa Rosa Junior College, CA; Lori Barkley, Portland State University, OR; Eileen Barlow, SUNY Albany, NY; Sue Bartch, Cuyahoga Community College, OH; Lora Bates, Oakton High School, VA; Nancy Baum, University of Texas at Arlington, TX; Linda Berendsen, Oakton Community College, IL; Jennifer Binckes Lee, Howard Community College, MD; Grace Bishop, Houston Community College, TX; Jean W. Bodman, Union County College, NJ; Virginia Bouchard, George Mason University, VA; Kimberley Briesch Sumner, University of Southern California, CA; Gabriela Cambiasso, Harold Washington College, IL; Jackie Campbell, Capistrano Unified School District, CA; Adele C. Camus, George Mason University, VA; Laura Chason, Savannah College, GA; Kerry Linder Catana, Language Studies International, NY; An Cheng, Oklahoma State University, OK; Carole Collins, North Hampton Community College, PA; Betty R. Compton, Intercultural Communications College, HI; Pamela Couch, Boston University, MA; Fernanda Crowe, Intrax International Institute, CA; Margo Czinski, Washtenaw Community College, MI; David Dahnke, Lone Star College, TX; Gillian M. Dale, CA; L. Dalgish, Concordia College, MN; Christopher Davis, John Jay College, NY; Sonia Delgadillo, Sierra College, CA; Marta O. Dmytrenko-Ahrabian, Wayne State University, MI; Javier Dominguez, Central High School, SC; Jo Ellen Downey-Greer, Lansing Community College, MI; Jennifer Duclos, Boston University, MA; Yvonne Duncan, City College of San Francisco, CA; Jennie Farnell, University of Connecticut, CT; Susan Fedors, Howard Community College, MD; Matthew Florence, Intrax International Institute, CA; Kathleen Flynn, Glendale College, CA; Eve Fonseca, St. Louis Community College, MO; Elizabeth Foss, Washtenaw Community College, MI; Duff C. Galda, Pima Community College, AZ; Christiane Galvani, Houston Community College, TX; Gretchen Gerber, Howard Community College, MD; Ray Gonzalez, Montgomery College, MD; Alyona Gorokhova, Grossmont College, CA; John Graney, Santa Fe College, FL; Kathleen Green, Central High School, AZ; Webb Hamilton, De Anza College, San Jose City College, CA; Janet Harclerode, Santa Monica Community College, CA; Sandra Hartmann, Language and Culture Center, TX; Kathy Haven, Mission College, CA; Adam Henricksen, University of Maryland, MD; Peter Hoffman, LaGuardia Community College, NY; Linda Holden, College of Lake County, IL; Jana Holt, Lake Washington Technical College, WA; Gail Ibele, University of Wisconsin, WI; Mandy Kama, Georgetown University, Washington, DC; Stephanie Kasuboski, Cuyahoga Community College, OH; Chigusa Katoku, Mission College, CA; Sandra Kawamura, Sacramento City College, CA; Gail Kellersberger, University of Houston, TX; Jane Kelly, Durham Technical Community College, NC; Julie Park Kim, George Mason University, VA; Lisa Kovacs-Morgan University of California, San Diego, CA; Claudia Kupiec, DePaul University, IL; Renee La Rue, Lone Star College-Montgomery, TX; Janet Langon, Glendale College, CA; Lawrence Lawson, Palomar College, CA; Rachele Lawton, The Community College of Baltimore County, MD; Alice Lee, Richland College, TX; Cherie Lenz-Hackett, University of Washington, WA; Joy Leventhal, Cuyahoga Community College, OH; Candace Lynch-Thompson, North Orange County Community College District, CA; Thi Thi Ma, City College of San Francisco, CA; Denise Maduli-Williams, City College of San Francisco, CA; Eileen Mahoney, Camelback High School, AZ; Brigitte Maronde, Harold Washington College, IL; Keith Maurice, University of Texas at Arlington, TX; Nancy Mayer, University of Missouri-St. Louis, MO; Karen Merritt, Glendale Union High School District, AZ; Holly Milkowart, Johnson County Community College, KS; Eric Moyer, Intrax International Institute, CA; Gino Muzzatti, Santa Rosa Junior College, CA; William Nedrow, Triton College, IL; Eric Nelson, University of Minnesota, MN; Rhony Ory, Ygnacio Valley High School, CA; Paul Parent, Montgomery College, MD; Oscar Pedroso, Miami Dade College, FL; Robin Persiani, Sierra College, CA; Patricia Prenz-Belkin, Hostos Community College, NY; Jim Ranalli, Iowa State University, IA; Toni R. Randall, Santa Monica College, CA; Vidya Rangachari, Mission College, CA; Elizabeth Rasmussen, Northern Virginia Community College, VA; Lara Ravitch, Truman College, IL; Deborah Repasz, San Jacinto College, TX; Andrey Reznikov, Black Hills State University, SD; Alison Rice, Hunter College, NY; Jennifer Robles, Ventura Unified School District, CA; Priscilla Rocha, Clark County School District, NV; Dzidra Rodins, DePaul University IL; Maria Rodriguez, Central High School, AZ; Maria Ruiz, Victor Valley College, CA; Kimberly Russell, Clark College, WA; Irene Sakk, Northwestern University, IL; Shaeley Santiago, Ames High School, IA; Peg Sarosy, San Francisco State University, CA; Alice Savage, North Harris College, TX; Donna Schaeffer, University of Washington, WA; Carol Schinger, Northern Virginia Community College, VA; Robert Scott, Kansas State University, KS; Suell Scott, Sheridan Technical Center, FL; Shira Seaman, Global English Academy, NY; Richard Seltzer, Glendale Community College, CA; Kathy Sherak, San Francisco State University, CA; German Silva, Miami Dade College, FL; Andrea Spector, Santa Monica Community College, CA; Karen Stanely, Central Piedmont Community College, NC; Ayse Stromsdorfer, Soldan I.S.H.S., MO; Yilin Sun, South Seattle Community College, WA; Thomas Swietlik, Intrax International Institute, IL; Judith Tanka, UCLA Extension–American Language Center, CA; Priscilla Taylor, University of Southern California, CA; Ilene Teixeira, Fairfax County Public Schools, VA; Shirl H. Terrell, Collin College, TX; Marya Teutsch-Dwyer, St. Cloud State University, MN; Stephen Thergesen, ELS Language Centers, CO; Christine Tierney, Houston Community College, TX; Arlene Turini, North Moore High School, NC; Suzanne Van Der Valk, Iowa State University, IA; Nathan D. Vasarhely, Ygnacio Valley High School, CA; Naomi S. Verratti, Howard Community College, MD; Hollyahna Vettori, Santa Rosa Junior College, CA; Laura Walsh, City College of San Francisco, CA; Andrew J. Watson, The English Bakery; Donald Weasenforth, Collin College, TX; Juliane Widner, Sheepshead Bay High School, NY; Lynne Wilkins, Mills College, CA; Dolores "Lorrie" Winter, California State University at Fullerton, CA; Jody Yamamoto, Kapi'olani Community College, HI; Ellen L. Yaniv, Boston University, MA; Norman Yoshida, Lewis & Clark College, OR; Joanna Zadra, American River College, CA; Florence Zysman, Santiago Canyon College, CA;

ASIA Rabiatu Abubakar, Eton Language Centre, Malaysia; Wiwik Andreani, Bina Nusantara University, Indonesia; Mike Baker, Kosei Junior High School, Japan; Leonard Barrow, Kanto Junior College, Japan; Herman Bartelen, Japan; Siren Betty, Fooyin University, Kaohsiung; Thomas E. Bieri, Nagoya College, Japan; Natalie Brezden, Global English House, Japan; MK Brooks, Mukogawa Women's University, Japan; Truong Ngoc Buu, The Youth Language School, Vietnam; Charles Cabell, Toyo University, Japan; Fred Carruth, Matsumoto University, Japan; Frances Causer, Seijo University, Japan; Deborah Chang, Wenzao Ursuline College of Languages, Kaohsiung; David Hindman Chatham, Ritsumeikan University, Japan; Andrew Chih Hong Chen, National Sun Yat-sen University, Kaohsiung; Christina Chen, Yu-Tsai Bilingual Elementary School, Taipei; Jason Jeffree Cole, Coto College, Japan; Le Minh Cong, Vungtau Tourism Vocational College, Vietnam; Todd Cooper, Toyama National College of Technology, Japan; Marie Cosgrove, Daito Bunka University, Japan; Tony Cripps, Ritsumeikan University, Japan; Daniel Cussen, Takushoku University, Japan; Le Dan, Ho Chi Minh City Electric Power College, Vietnam; Simon Daykin, Banghwa-dong Community Centre, South Korea; Aimee Denham, ILA, Vietnam; Bryan Dickson, David's English Center, Taipei; Nathan Ducker, Japan University, Japan; Ian Duncan, Simul International Corporate Training, Japan; Nguyen Thi Kieu Dung, Thang Long University, Vietnam; Nguyen Thi Thuy Duong, Vietnamese American Vocational Training College, Vietnam; Wong Tuck Ee, Raja Tun Azlan Science Secondary School, Malaysia; Emilia Effendy, International Islamic University Malaysia, Malaysia; Robert Eva, Kaisei Girls High School, Japan; Jim George, Luna International Language School, Japan; Jurgen Germeys, Silk Road Language Center, South Korea; Wong Ai Gnoh, SMJK Chung Hwa Confucian, Malaysia; Peter Goosselink, Hokkai High School,

Japan; **Wendy M. Gough**, St. Mary College/Nunoike Gaigo Senmon Gakko, Japan; **Tim Grose**, Sapporo Gakuin University, Japan; **Pham Thu Ha**, Le Van Tam Primary School, Vietnam; **Ann-Marie Hadzima**, Taipei; **Troy Hammond**, Tokyo Gakugei University International Secondary School, Japan; **Robiatul 'Adawiah Binti Hamzah**, SMK Putrajaya Precinct 8(1), Malaysia; **Tran Thi Thuy Hang**, Ho Chi Minh City Banking University, Vietnam; **To Thi Hong Hanh**, CEFALT, Vietnam; **Janis Hearn**, Hongik University, South Korea; **David Hindman**, Sejong University, South Korea; **Nahn Cam Hoa**, Ho Chi Minh City University of Technology, Vietnam; **Jana Holt**, Korea University, South Korea; **Jason Hollowell**, Nihon University, Japan; **F. N. (Zoe) Hsu**, National Tainan University, Yong Kang; **Wenhua Hsu**, I-Shou University, Kaohsiung; **Luu Nguyen Quoc Hung,** Cantho University, Vietnam ; **Cecile Hwang**, Changwon National University, South Korea; **Ainol Haryati Ibrahim**, Universiti Malaysia Pahang, Malaysia; **Robert Jeens**, Yonsei University, South Korea; **Linda M. Joyce**, Kyushu Sangyo University, Japan; **Dr. Nisai Kaewsanchai**, English Square Kanchanaburi, Thailand; **Aniza Kamarulzaman**, Sabah Science Secondary School, Malaysia; **Ikuko Kashiwabara**, Osaka Electro-Communication University, Japan; **Gurmit Kaur**, INTI College, Malaysia; **Nick Keane**, Japan; **Ward Ketcheson,** Aomori University, Japan; **Montchatry Ketmuni**, Rajamangala University of Technology, Thailand; **Dinh Viet Khanh**, Vietnam; **Seonok Kim**, Kangsu Jongro Language School, South Korea; **Kelly P. Kimura**, Soka University, Japan; **Stan Kirk**, Konan University, Japan; **Donald Knight**, Nan Hua/Fu Li Junior High Schools, Hsinchu; **Kari J. Kostiainen**, Nagoya City University, Japan; **Pattri Kuanpulpol**, Silpakorn University, Thailand; **Ha Thi Lan**, Thai Binh Teacher Training College, Vietnam; **Eric Edwin Larson**, Miyazaki Prefectural Nursing University, Japan; **Richard S. Lavin**, Prefectural University of Kumamoto, Japan; **Shirley Leane**, Chugoku Junior College, Japan; **Tae Lee**, Yonsei University, South Korea; **Lys Yongsoon Lee**, Reading Town Geumcheon, South Korea; **Mallory Leece**, Sun Moon University, South Korea; **Dang Hong Lien**, Tan Lam Upper Secondary School, Vietnam; **Huang Li-Han**, Rebecca Education Institute, Taipei; **Sovannarith Lim**, Royal University of Phnom Penh, Cambodia; **Ginger Lin**, National Kaohsiung Hospitality College, Kaohsiung; **Noel Lineker**, New Zealand/Japan; **Tran Dang Khanh Linh**, Nha Trang Teachers' Training College, Vietnam; **Daphne Liu**, Buliton English School, Taipei; **S. F. Josephine Liu**, Tien-Mu Elementary School, Taipei ; **Caroline Luo**, Tunghai University, Taichung; **Jeng-Jia Luo**, Tunghai University, Taichung; **Laura MacGregor**, Gakushuin University, Japan; **Amir Madani**, Visuttharangsi School, Thailand; **Elena Maeda**, Sacred Heart Professional Training College, Japan; **Vu Thi Thanh Mai**, Hoang Gia Education Center, Vietnam; **Kimura Masakazu**, Kato Gakuen Gyoshu High School, Japan; **Susumu Matsuhashi**, Net Link English School, Japan; **James McCrostie**, Daito Bunka University, Japan; **Joel McKee**, Inha University, South Korea; **Colin McKenzie**, Wachirawit Primary School, Thailand; **William K. Moore**, Hiroshima Kokusai Gakuin University, Japan; **Hudson Murrell**, Baiko Gakuin University, Japan; **Frances Namba**, Senri International School of Kwansei Gakuin, Japan; **Keiichi Narita**, Niigata University, Japan; **Kim Chung Nguyen**, Ho Chi Minh University of Industry, Vietnam; **Do Thi Thanh Nhan**, Hanoi University, Vietnam; **Dale Kazuo Nishi**, Aoyama English Conversation School, Japan; **Louise Ohashi**, Shukutoku University, Japan; **Virgina Peng**, Ritsumeikan University, Japan; **Suangkanok Piboonthamnont**, Rajamangala University of Technology, Thailand; **Simon Pitcher**, Business English Teaching Services, Japan; **John C. Probert**, New Education Worldwide, Thailand; **Do Thi Hoa Quyen**, Ton Duc Thang University, Vietnam; **John P. Racine**, Dokkyo University, Japan; **Kevin Ramsden**, Kyoto University of Foreign Studies, Japan; **Luis Rappaport**, Cung Thieu Nha Ha Noi, Vietnam; **Lisa Reshad**, Konan Daigaku Hyogo, Japan; **Peter Riley**, Taisho University, Japan; **Thomas N. Robb**, Kyoto Sangyo University, Japan; **Maria Feti Rosyani,** Universitas Kristen Indonesia, Indonesia; **Greg Rouault**, Konan University, Japan; **Chris Ruddenklau**, Kindai University, Japan; **Hans-Gustav Schwartz**, Thailand; **Mary-Jane Scott**, Soongsil University, South Korea; **Jenay Seymour,** Hongik University, South Korea; **James Sherlock**, A.P.W. Angthong, Thailand; **Yuko Shimizu**, Ritsumeikan University, Japan; **Suzila Mohd Shukor**, Universiti Sains Malaysia, Malaysia; **Stephen E. Smith**, Mahidol University, Thailand; **Mi-young Song**, Kyungwon University, South Korea; **Jason Stewart**, Taejon International Language School, South Korea; **Brian A. Stokes**, Korea University, South Korea; **Mulder Su**, Shih-Chien University, Kaohsiung;

Yoomi Suh, English Plus, South Korea; **Yun-Fang Sun**, Wenzao Ursuline College of Languages, Kaohsiung; **Richard Swingle**, Kansai Gaidai University, Japan; **Tran Hoang Tan**, School of International Training, Vietnam; **Takako Tanaka**, Doshisha University, Japan; **Jeffrey Taschner**, American University Alumni Language Center, Thailand ; **Michael Taylor**, International Pioneers School, Thailand; **Tran Duong The**, Sao Mai Language Center, Vietnam; **Tran Dinh Tho**, Duc Tri Secondary School, Vietnam; **Huynh Thi Anh Thu**, Nhatrang College of Culture Arts and Tourism, Vietnam; **Peter Timmins**, Peter's English School, Japan; **Fumie Togano**, Hosei Daini High School, Japan; **F. Sigmund Topor**, Keio University Language School, Japan; **Yen-Cheng Tseng**, Chang-Jung Christian University, Tainan; **Hajime Uematsu**, Hirosaki University, Japan; **Rachel Um**, Mok-dong Oedae English School, South Korea; **David Underhill**, EEExpress, Japan; **Siriluck Usaha**, Sripatum University, Thailand; **Tyas Budi Utami**, Indonesia; **Nguyen Thi Van**, Far East International School, Vietnam; **Stephan Van Eycken**, Kosei Gakuen Girls High School, Japan; **Zisa Velasquez**, Taihu International School/Semarang International School, China/Indonesia; **Jeffery Walter**, Sangji University, South Korea; **Bill White**, Kinki University, Japan; **Yohanes De Deo Widyastoko**, Xaverius Senior High School, Indonesia; **Greg Chung-Hsien Wu**, Providence University, Taichung; **Hui-Lien Yeh**, Chai Nan University of Pharmacy and Science, Tainan; **Sittiporn Yodnil**, Huachiew Chalermprakiet University, Thailand; **Shamshul Helmy Zambahari**, Universiti Teknologi Malaysia, Malaysia; **Aimin Fadhlee bin Mahmud Zuhodi**, Kuala Terengganu Science School, Malaysia;

TURKEY **Seval Akmeşe**, Haliç University; **Gül Akkoç**, Boğaziçi University; **Deniz Balım**, Haliç University; **Robert Ledbury**, Izmir University of Economics; **Oya Özağaç**, Boğaziçi University;

THE MIDDLE EAST **Amina Saif Mohammed Al Hashamia**, Nizwa College of Applied Sciences, Oman; **Sharon Ruth Devaneson**, Ibri College of Technology, Oman; **Hanaa El-Deeb,** Canadian International College, Egypt; **Brian Gay**, Sultan Qaboos University, Oman; **Gail Al-Hafidh**, Sharjah Higher Colleges of Technology, U.A.E.; **Jonathan Hastings**, American Language Center, Jordan; **Sian Khoury**, Fujairah Women's College (HCT), U.A.E.; **Jessica March**, American University of Sharjah, U.A.E.; **Neil McBeath**, Sultan Qaboos University, Oman;

LATIN AMERICA **Aldana Aguirre**, Argentina; **Claudia Almeida**, Coordenação de Idiomas, Brazil; **Cláudia Arias**, Brazil; **Maria de los Angeles Barba**, FES Acatlan UNAM, Mexico; **Lilia Barrios**, Universidad Autónoma de Tamaulipas, Mexico; **Adán Beristain**, UAEM, Mexico; **Ricardo Böck**, Manoel Ribas, Brazil; **Edson Braga**, CNA, Brazil; **Marli Buttelli**, Mater et Magistra, Brazil; **Alessandra Campos**, Inova Centro de Linguas, Brazil; **Priscila Catta Preta Ribeiro**, Brazil; **Gustavo Cestari**, Access International School, Brazil; **Walter D'Alessandro**, Virginia Language Center, Brazil; **Lilian De Gennaro**, Argentina; **Mônica De Stefani**, Quality Centro de Idiomas, Brazil; **Julio Alejandro Flores**, BUAP, Mexico; **Mirian Freire**, CNA Vila Guilherme, Brazil; **Francisco Garcia**, Colegio Lestonnac de San Angel, Mexico; **Miriam Giovanardi**, Brazil; **Darlene Gonzalez Miy**, ITESM CCV, Mexico; **Maria Laura Grimaldi**, Argentina; **Luz Dary Guzmán**, IMPAHU, Colombia; **Carmen Koppe**, Brazil; **Monica Krutzler**, Brazil; **Marcus Murilo Lacerda**, Seven Idiomas, Brazil; **Nancy Lake**, CEL-LEP, Brazil; **Cris Lazzerini**, Brazil; **Sandra Luna**, Argentina; **Ricardo Luvisan**, Brazil; **Jorge Murilo Menezes**, ACBEU, Brazil; **Monica Navarro**, Instituto Cultural A. C., Mexico; **Joacyr Oliveira**, Faculdades Metropolitanas Unidas and Summit School for Teachers, Brazil; **Ayrton Cesar Oliveira de Araujo**, E&A English Classes, Brazil; **Ana Laura Oriente**, Seven Idiomas, Brazil; **Adelia Peña Clavel**, CELE UNAM, Mexico; **Beatriz Pereira**, Summit School, Brazil; **Miguel Perez**, Instituto Cultural Mexico; **Cristiane Perone**, Associação Cultura Inglesa, Brazil; **Pamela Claudia Pogré**, Colegio Integral Caballito/ Universidad de Flores, Argentina; **Dalva Prates**, Brazil; **Marianne Rampaso**, Iowa Idiomas, Brazil; **Daniela Rutolo**, Instituto Superior Cultural Británico, Argentina; **Maione Sampaio**, Maione Carrijo Consultoria em Inglês Ltda, Brazil; **Elaine Santesso**, TS Escola de Idiomas, Brazil; **Camila Francisco Santos**, UNS Idiomas, Brazil; **Lucia Silva**, Cooplem Idiomas, Brazil; **Maria Adela Sorzio**, Instituto Superior Santa Cecilia, Argentina; **Elcio Souza**, Unibero, Brazil; **Willie Thomas**, Rainbw Idiomas, Brazil; **Sandra Villegas**, Instituto Humberto de Paolis, Argentina; **John Whelan**, La Universidad Nacional Autonoma de Mexico, Mexico

WELCOME TO Q:Skills for Success

Q: Skills for Success is a six-level series with two strands,
Reading and Writing and *Listening and Speaking*.

READING AND WRITING

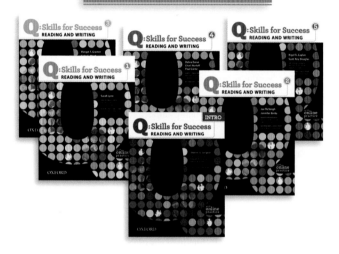

LISTENING AND SPEAKING

WITH Q ONLINE PRACTICE

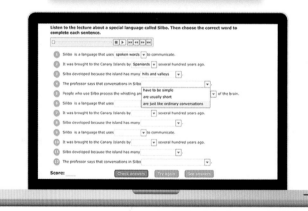

STUDENT AND TEACHER INFORMED

Q: Skills for Success is the result of an extensive development process involving thousands of teachers and hundreds of students around the world. Their views and opinions helped shape the content of the series. *Q* is grounded in teaching theory as well as real-world classroom practice, making it the most learner-centered series available.

CONTENTS

Q connects critical thinking, language skills, and learning outcomes.

LANGUAGE SKILLS

Explicit skills instruction enables students to meet their academic and professional goals.

LEARNING OUTCOMES

Clearly identified **learning outcomes** focus students on the goal of their instruction.

UNIT 5
Responsibility

READING	using a graphic organizer
VOCABULARY	phrasal verbs
WRITING	stating reasons and giving examples
GRAMMAR	gerunds and infinitives

LEARNING OUTCOME
Write a paragraph about why people help others using reasons and examples.

Unit QUESTION

Why do people help each other?

PREVIEW THE UNIT

Ⓐ Discuss these questions with your classmates.

Did your parents teach you to be helpful to others? Is being helpful something we learn, or is it human nature?

Are there any situations in which you don't think you should help someone? Explain.

Look at the photo. What do you think is happening?

Ⓑ Discuss the Unit Question above with your classmates.

Listen to *The Q Classroom*, Track 2 on CD 2, to hear other answers.

88   UNIT 5   89

CRITICAL THINKING

Thought-provoking **unit questions** engage students with the topic and provide a **critical thinking framework** for the unit.

 Having the learning outcome is important because it gives students and teachers a clear idea of what the point of each task/activity in the unit is.
Lawrence Lawson, Palomar College, California

LANGUAGE SKILLS

Two reading texts provide input on the unit question and give **exposure to academic content.**

The Biology of Altruism

1   Scientific evidence suggests that humans have a biological desire to help others, including strangers. **Altruistic** behavior towards strangers is uniquely human and observed at a very young age. Dr. Felix Warneken and Dr. Michael Tomasello of Germany's Max Planck Institute for Evolutionary Anthropology have shown that children as young as 18 months want to help strangers. When their 18-month-old **subjects** saw a stranger throw a pencil on the floor, none of them picked it up. However, when the same subjects saw someone "accidentally" drop a pencil, nearly all the children picked it up in the first ten seconds. Says Dr. Warneken, "The results were astonishing because these children are so young. They still wear diapers and are **barely** able to use language, but they already show helping behavior." Because altruistic behavior appears in children so young, Dr. Warneken and other scientists **hypothesize** that the human brain is designed to be altruistic.

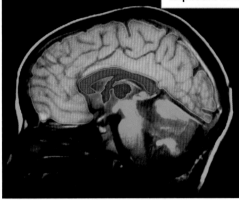
Brain scans like this one help scientists see the brain in action.

cry or smile when someone smiles at us. Our mirror neurons actually feel what they feel. They cry and smile along with them.

3   How, then, can mirror neurons **bring about** altruistic behavior? By helping us feel what others feel, mirror neurons naturally make us feel **compassionate**. They allow us to put ourselves in someone else's situation; without them, we would not understand or

CRITICAL THINKING

Students **discuss** their opinions of each reading text and **analyze** how it changes their perspective on the unit question.

 **WHAT DO YOU THINK?**

A. Discuss the questions in a group.

1. How altruistic do you think you are? Give examples to support your opinion.

2. Why do you think some people are more altruistic than others?

 One of the best features is your focus on developing materials of a high "interest level."
Troy Hammond, Tokyo Gakugei University, International Secondary School, Japan

Explicit skills instruction prepares students for academic success.

LANGUAGE SKILLS

Explicit instruction and practice in reading, vocabulary, grammar and writing skills **help students achieve language proficiency.**

LEARNING OUTCOMES

Practice activities allow students to **master the skills** before they are evaluated at the end of the unit.

Q WHAT DO YOU THINK?

Discuss the questions in a group. Then choose one question and write five to eight sentences in response.

1. Have you ever *not* helped someone who needed help? Why or why not? What factors might make someone choose not to help a stranger?

2. In general, which people do you think are more helpful to strangers in need: people who live in cities or people who live in small towns? Why?

3. The author of "A Question of Numbers" writes that "some cultures might put more importance on helping strangers than others do." Do you think that a person's culture can be a factor in making him or her a more helpful person? Why or why not?

Reading Skill | **Using a graphic organizer**

Graphic organizers represent ideas with images, such as diagrams, charts, tables, and timelines. You can use graphic organizers to help you see connections between ideas or remember the main points of a text or parts of a text. Using graphic organizers can help you review a text you have read in preparation for class or a test.

The flowchart below organizes the main points of a scientific article.

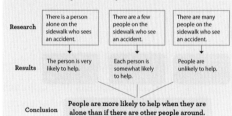

WRITING

Writing Skill | **Using descriptive adjectives**

Adjectives are words that describe nouns (*people*, *places*, *things*, and *ideas*). Writers use a lot of adjectives in order to make their descriptions both interesting and clear. They describe what they *see*, *hear*, *smell*, *taste*, *touch*, and *feel*. They paint a picture with words so that readers can easily imagine or "see" what they are describing. Using **descriptive adjectives** in your writing will make it more interesting for the reader.

> **Non-descriptive:** I ate a meal at a restaurant downtown.
> **Descriptive:** I ate a **delicious**, **savory** meal at a **cozy French** restaurant downtown.

A. Read the paragraph. Then answer the questions with a partner.

My Mother's Yorkshire Pudding

Whenever I think of my mother's cooking, I always remember her delicious Yorkshire puddings. Although I grew up in the United States, my mother often cooked dishes from her home country of England. She has always been an excellent cook, and one of her best recipes is called Yorkshire pudding, which is a traditional English pastry. It is a simple dish made with eggs, flour, and milk. My mother's Yorkshire puddings taste so good because they are light, crisp, and slightly sweet. She serves them with delicious warm gravy, but I prefer them sweet with strawberry jam. They are very special because she only serves them on holidays. My sister and I always fight for the last one because they are so delicious. I have had many other people's Yorkshire puddings, but my mother's have always tasted better. Not only are hers homemade, but they also have a special taste that always makes me think of her. They also make me remember my British ancestry and my mother's history. They help me connect to my past and to my family. Yorkshire pudding is such a simple and common English food, but it will always be special to me because of my mother.

1. What is the topic sentence? Underline it.

2. What is the concluding sentence? Underline it.

3. How does Yorkshire pudding taste? Circle the sentence that describes the taste.

  The tasks are simple, accessible, user-friendly, and very useful.
Jessica March, American University of Sharjah, U.A.E.

Q Online Practice provides all new content for additional practice in an easy-to-use online workbook. Every student book includes a *Q Online Practice access code card*. Use the access code to register for your *Q Online Practice* account at www.Qonlinepractice.com.

Vocabulary Skill **Using the dictionary**

Word Forms

Learning word forms increases your vocabulary. It will help make your reading, speaking, and writing more fluent. Look at the dictionary definitions below.

ac·com·plish /ə'kɑmplɪʃ/ *verb* [T] to succeed in doing something difficult that you planned to do: *Very little was accomplished at the meeting.* **SYN** achieve

ac·com·plished /ə'kɑmplɪʃt/ *adj.* highly skilled at something: *an accomplished pianist*

ac·com·plish·ment /ə'kɑmplɪʃmənt/ *noun* **1** [C] something difficult that someone has succeeded in doing or learning: *He was proud of his academic accomplishments.* **2** (*formal*) [U] the act of completing something successfully

All dictionary entries are taken from the *Oxford American Dictionary for learners of English.*

A **research-based vocabulary program** focuses students on the words they need to know academically and professionally, using skill strategies based on the same research as the Oxford dictionaries.

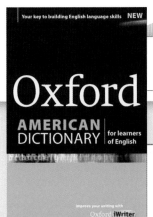

All dictionary entries are taken from the *Oxford American Dictionary for learners of English.*

The *Oxford American Dictionary for learners of English* was developed with English learners in mind, and provides extra learning tools for pronunciation, verb types, basic grammar structures, and more.

The Oxford 3000™
The Oxford 3000 encompasses **the 3000 most important words to learn in English.** It is based on a comprehensive analysis of the Oxford English Corpus, a two billion word collection of English text, and on extensive research with both language and pedagogical experts.

The Academic Word List AWL
The Academic Word List was created by Averil Coxhead and contains **570 words that are commonly used in academic English,** such as in textbooks or articles across a wide range of academic subject areas. These words are a great place to start if you are studying English for academic purposes.

Clear learning outcomes focus students on the goals of instruction.

LEARNING OUTCOMES

A culminating unit assignment evaluates the students' **mastery of the learning outcome.**

Unit Assignment | **Write a paragraph with reasons and examples**

 In this assignment, you are going to write a paragraph with reasons and examples. As you prepare your paragraph, think about the Unit Question, "Why do people help each other?" Refer to the Self-Assessment checklist on page 110. Use information from Readings 1 and 2 and your work in this unit to support your ideas.

For alternative unit assignments, see the *Q: Skills for Success Teacher's Handbook.*

PLAN AND WRITE

A. BRAINSTORM In a group, brainstorm reasons other than than the ones in the readings that might affect a person's decision to help others. Write your ideas in your notebook.

B. PLAN Follow these steps as you plan your paragraph.

1. Look at your notes from Activity A. Circle the reasons you want to include in your paragraph. Then think of examples to support these reasons.

2. Think about the readings in this unit. Is there any information from them that can help support your ideas?

LEARNER CENTERED

Track Your Success allows students to **assess their own progress** and provides guidance on remediation.

Check (✓) the skills you learned. If you need more work on a skill, refer to the page(s) in parentheses.

READING	I can use a graphic organizer. (p. 96)
VOCABULARY	I can use phrasal verbs. (p. 103)
WRITING	I can state reasons and give examples. (p. 105)
GRAMMAR	I can use gerunds and infinitives. (p. 107)
LEARNING OUTCOME	I can write a paragraph about why people help others using reasons and examples.

 Students can check their learning ... and they can focus on the essential points when they study.

Suh Yoomi, Seoul, South Korea

Q Online Practice

For the student

- **Easy-to-use:** a simple interface allows students to focus on enhancing their speaking and listening skills, not learning a new software program
- **Flexible:** for use anywhere there's an Internet connection
- **Access code card:** a *Q Online Practice* access code is included with this book—use the access code to register for *Q Online Practice* at www.Qonlinepractice.com

For the teacher

- **Simple yet powerful:** automatically grades student exercises and tracks progress
- **Straightforward:** online management system to review, print, or export reports
- **Flexible:** for use in the classroom or easily assigned as homework
- **Access code card:** contact your sales rep for your *Q Online Practice* teacher's access code

Teacher Resources

Q Teacher's Handbook gives strategic support through:

- specific teaching notes for each activity
- ideas for ensuring student participation
- multilevel strategies and expansion activities
- the answer key
- special sections on 21st Century Skills and critical thinking
- a *Testing Program CD-ROM* with a customizable test for each unit

For additional resources visit the *Q: Skills for Success* companion website at www.oup.com/elt/teacher/Qskillsforsuccess

Q Class Audio includes:

- reading texts
- *The Q Classroom*

> It's an interesting, engaging series which provides plenty of materials that are easy to use in class, as well as instructionally promising.
> *Donald Weasenforth, Collin College, Texas*

UNIT	READING	WRITING
1 **First Impressions** **How do you make a good first impression?** **READING 1:** How to Make a Strong First Impression A Magazine Article (Interpersonal Communication) **READING 2:** Job Interviews 101 A Magazine Article (Jobs and Work)	• Preview text using a variety of strategies • Read for main ideas • Read for details • Use glosses and footnotes to aid reading comprehension • Read and recognize different text types • Fill out a questionnaire to anticipate content of reading • Identify main ideas and supporting details	• Write paragraphs of different genres • Plan before writing • Revise, edit, and rewrite • Give feedback to peers and self-assess • Develop a paragraph: topic sentence, supporting sentences, concluding sentence • Make an outline • Write a "how to" paragraph
2 **Food and Taste** **What makes food taste good?** **READING 1:** Knowing Your Tastes A Magazine Article (Food) **READING 2:** Finding Balance in Food An Online Magazine Article (Nutrition)	• Preview text using a variety of strategies • Read for main ideas • Read for details • Use glosses and footnotes to aid reading comprehension • Read and recognize different text types • Take a quiz to anticipate content of reading • Analyze the structure of a text as a previewing strategy • Use prior knowledge to predict content	• Write paragraphs of different genres • Plan before writing • Revise, edit, and rewrite • Give feedback to peers and self-assess • Use descriptive adjectives • Write a descriptive paragraph
3 **Success** **What does it take to be successful?** **READING 1:** Fast Cars, Big Money A Magazine Article (Business) **READING 2:** Practice Makes … Pain? An Online Article (Sports and Competition)	• Preview text using a variety of strategies • Read for main ideas • Read for details • Use glosses and footnotes to aid reading comprehension • Read and recognize different text types • Complete a survey to anticipate content of reading • Use an idea map to activate schema • Use headings to determine the purpose of a text • Scan to find specific information such as names, numbers, and dates • Use titles to predict content	• Write paragraphs of different genres • Plan before writing • Revise, edit, and rewrite • Give feedback to peers and self-assess • Formulate opinions, reasons, and examples • Write an opinion paragraph

VOCABULARY	GRAMMAR	CRITICAL THINKING	UNIT OUTCOME
• Match definitions • Define new terms • Learn selected vocabulary words from the Oxford 3000 and the Academic Word List • Use the dictionary to identify word forms	• Real conditionals: present and future	• Reflect on the unit • Connect ideas across texts or readings • Express ideas/reactions/opinions orally and in writing • Relate information from unit to self • Set and achieve goals • Apply unit tips and use *Q Online Practice* to become a strategic learner • Complete a T-chart to categorize information • Analyze ways to make a good first impression	• Develop a "how to" paragraph that details the steps involved in making a good impression.
• Match definitions • Define new terms • Learn selected vocabulary words from the Oxford 3000 and the Academic Word List • Use context to understand unfamiliar vocabulary	• Ordering of adjectives	• Reflect on the unit • Connect ideas across texts or readings • Express ideas/reactions/opinions orally and in writing • Relate information from unit to self • Set and achieve goals • Apply unit tips and use *Q Online Practice* to become a strategic learner • Fill in a chart to categorize information • Evaluate qualities of food	• Write a paragraph about your favorite dish using descriptive adjectives.
• Match definitions • Define new terms • Learn selected vocabulary words from the Oxford 3000 and the Academic Word List • Recognize and use adjective + preposition collocations to expand vocabulary	• Subject-verb agreement	• Reflect on the unit • Connect ideas across texts or readings • Express ideas/reactions/opinions orally and in writing • Relate information from unit to self • Set and achieve goals • Apply unit tips and use *Q Online Practice* to become a strategic learner • Fill in a chart to categorize information • Evaluate the elements of personal success	• State and support your personal perspectives in an "opinion" paragraph.

UNIT	READING	WRITING
4 New Perspectives **How has technology affected your life?** **READING 1:** Having a Second Life A Computer Magazine Article (Social Networking) **READING 2:** Living Outside the Box An Online Newspaper Article (Technology)	• Preview text using a variety of strategies • Read for main ideas • Read for details • Use glosses and footnotes to aid reading comprehension • Read and recognize different text types • Complete a questionnaire to anticipate content of reading • Take notes while reading to be an active reader • Use title and photos to predict content	• Write paragraphs of different genres • Plan before writing • Revise, edit, and rewrite • Give feedback to peers and self-assess • Analyze features of good/poor summaries • Write a summary • Write a personal response to the unit question
5 Responsibility **Why do people help each other?** **READING 1:** A Question of Numbers A News Magazine Article (Psychology) **READING 2:** The Biology of Altruism A Science Journal Article (Biology)	• Preview text using a variety of strategies • Read for main ideas • Read for details • Use glosses and footnotes to aid reading comprehension • Read and recognize different text types • Use pictures to activate schema and predict content • Make predictions about text • Use graphic organizers to review and aid comprehension	• Write paragraphs of different genres • Plan before writing • Revise, edit, and rewrite • Give feedback to peers and self-assess • State reasons and give examples to support ideas in writing • Use *because* to state reasons • Write a paragraph with reasons and examples
6 Advertising **Does advertising help or harm us?** **READING 1:** Happiness is in the Shoes You Wear A News Magazine Article (Advertising) **READING 2:** In Defense of Advertising An Article Based on a Canadian Radio Show (Business)	• Preview text using a variety of strategies • Read for main ideas • Read for details • Use glosses and footnotes to aid reading comprehension • Read and recognize different text types • Use photos to activate schema and anticipate content • Make predictions about text • Distinguish fact from opinion to be a critical reader • Use prior knowledge to predict content	• Write paragraphs of different genres • Plan before writing • Revise, edit, and rewrite • Give feedback to peers and self-assess • Write introduction, body, and concluding paragraphs • Write a letter to the editor based on the unit question
7 Risk **Why do people take risks?** **READING 1:** Fear Factor: Success and Risk in Extreme Sports An Article from *National Geographic News* (Psychology) **READING 2:** The Climb of My Life An Excerpt from a Book (Extreme Sports)	• Preview text using a variety of strategies • Read for main ideas • Read for details • Use glosses and footnotes to aid reading comprehension • Read and recognize different text types • Use photos to activate schema and anticipate content • Identify and use referents in text to understand contrast • Make predictions about text • Sequence ideas to show text structure • Use prior knowledge to predict content	• Write paragraphs of different genres • Plan before writing • Revise, edit, and rewrite • Give feedback to peers and self-assess • Write a multi-paragraph narrative essay with the focus on the introductory paragraph

VOCABULARY	GRAMMAR	CRITICAL THINKING	UNIT OUTCOME
• Match definitions • Define new terms • Learn selected vocabulary words from the Oxford 3000 and the Academic Word List • Learn and use synonyms to expand vocabulary and add variety to writing	• Parallel structure	• Reflect on the unit • Connect ideas across texts or readings • Express ideas/reactions/opinions orally and in writing • Relate information from unit to self • Set and achieve goals • Apply unit tips and use *Q Online Practice* to become a strategic learner • Compare and contrast information presented in a chart • Formulate an opinion	• Write a paragraph summarizing a reading text and an opinion paragraph in response to the text.
• Match definitions • Define new terms • Learn selected vocabulary words from the Oxford 3000 and the Academic Word List • Learn and use phrasal verbs to expand vocabulary	• Gerunds and infinitives	• Reflect on the unit • Connect ideas across texts or readings • Express ideas/reactions/opinions orally and in writing • Relate information from unit to self • Set and achieve goals • Apply unit tips and use *Q Online Practice* to become a strategic learner • Use a graphic organizer to see connections between ideas and patterns of organization • Determine what makes people help each other	• Write a paragraph about why people help others using reasons and examples.
• Match definitions • Define new terms • Learn selected vocabulary words from the Oxford 3000 and the Academic Word List • Learn and use suffixes to change word forms and expand vocabulary	• Compound sentences with *and, but, so,* and *or*	• Reflect on the unit • Connect ideas across texts or readings • Express ideas/reactions/opinions orally and in writing • Relate information from unit to self • Set and achieve goals • Apply unit tips and use *Q Online Practice* to become a strategic learner • Fill in a chart to categorize information • Formulate and justify an opinion	• Write a multiple-paragraph letter to the editor expressing your opinion about advertising.
• Match definitions • Define new terms • Learn selected vocabulary words from the Oxford 3000 and the Academic Word List • Use the dictionary to find and use the correct definition of words with multiple meanings	• Shifts between past and present in narrative writing	• Reflect on the unit • Connect ideas across texts or readings • Express ideas/reactions/opinions orally and in writing • Relate information from unit to self • Set and achieve goals • Apply unit tips and use *Q Online Practice* to become a strategic learner • Rank and justify rankings • Analyze and describe a previous personal risk	• Develop a narrative essay describing a risk you have taken.

UNIT	READING	WRITING
8 Cities/Urban Lives **How can we make cities better places to live?** **READING 1: New Zero-Carbon City to be Built** A News Website Article (Environmental Science) **READING 2: "Out of the Box" Ideas for Greener Cities** A News Magazine Article (City Planning)	• Preview text using a variety of strategies • Read for main ideas • Read for details • Use glosses and footnotes to aid reading comprehension • Read and recognize different text types • Take a quiz to anticipate content of reading • Make predictions about text • Make inferences to maximize comprehension	• Write paragraphs of different genres • Plan before writing • Revise, edit, and rewrite • Give feedback to peers and self-assess • Write a problem/solution essay with the focus on the thesis statement
9 Money **How can a small amount of money make a big difference?** **READING 1: How a Ugandan Girl Got an Education** A News Magazine Article (Charity) **READING 2: Money Makes You Happy— If You Spend It on Others** A News Website Article (Psychology)	• Preview text using a variety of strategies • Read for main ideas • Read for details • Use glosses and footnotes to aid reading comprehension • Read and recognize different text types • Use photos to activate schema and anticipate content • Use a timeline to determine the sequence of events • Make predictions about text	• Write paragraphs of different genres • Plan before writing • Revise, edit, and rewrite • Give feedback to peers and self-assess • Write a cause/effect essay with the focus on body paragraphs
10 Communication **Do people communicate better now than in the past?** **READING 1: 2B or not 2B?** A Newspaper Article (Communication Studies) **READING 2: Social Networking Sites: Are They Changing Human Communication?** A Magazine Article (Social Networking)	• Preview text using a variety of strategies • Read for main ideas • Read for details • Use glosses and footnotes to aid reading comprehension • Read and recognize different text types • Complete a survey to anticipate content of reading • Order details to determine sequence in text • Identify the author's purpose, audience, and tone • Use prior knowledge to predict content • Skim text for main idea	• Write paragraphs of different genres • Plan before writing • Revise, edit, and rewrite • Give feedback to peers and self-assess • Write an opinion essay with the focus on counterarguments and the concluding paragraph

VOCABULARY	GRAMMAR	CRITICAL THINKING	UNIT OUTCOME
• Match definitions • Define new terms • Learn selected vocabulary words from the Oxford 3000 and the Academic Word List • Recognize and use participial adjectives to expand vocabulary	• Passive voice	• Reflect on the unit • Connect ideas across texts or readings • Express ideas/reactions/opinions orally and in writing • Relate information from unit to self • Set and achieve goals • Apply unit tips and use *Q Online Practice* to become a strategic learner • Categorize advantages in a chart • Identify a problem and formulate solutions	• Write a problem/solution essay describing how your city can become a better place to live.
• Match definition • Define new terms • Learn selected vocabulary words from the Oxford 3000 and the Academic Word List • Learn and use noun collocations to expand vocabulary	• Complex sentences	• Reflect on the unit • Connect ideas across texts or readings • Express ideas/reactions/opinions orally and in writing • Relate information from unit to self • Set and achieve goals • Apply unit tips and use *Q Online Practice* to become a strategic learner • Complete a graphic organizer to show cause/effect • Assess a situation and interpret cause and affect	• Write a cause/effect essay explaining how a small amount of money can make a big difference.
• Match definitions • Define new terms • Learn selected vocabulary words from the Oxford 3000 and the Academic Word List • Use prefixes to guess meaning of new vocabulary	• Sentence fragments	• Reflect on the unit • Connect ideas across texts or readings • Express ideas/reactions/opinions orally and in writing • Relate information from unit to self • Set and achieve goals • Apply unit tips and use *Q Online Practice* to become a strategic learner • Recognize arguments and counterarguments • State an opinon and justify it with reasons and examples	• Develop an essay about communication that states your personal opinion and gives a counterargument.

UNIT

1

First Impressions

READING ● identifying main ideas and supporting details
VOCABULARY ● using the dictionary
WRITING ● organizing and developing a paragraph
GRAMMAR ● real conditionals: present and future

Unit QUESTION

How do you make a good first impression?

PREVIEW THE UNIT

A **Discuss these questions with your classmates.**

What qualities do you look for in a friend?

What is the best way to make a good first impression on a classmate? On a boss?

Look at the photo. What are the people doing? Why?

B **Discuss the Unit Question above with your classmates.**

Listen to *The Q Classroom*, Track 2 on CD 1, to hear other answers.

C Look at the questionnaire. Choose the answer that makes each statement true for you.

Do You Make a Good First Impression?

1. **When I talk to someone I don't know, …**
   - ○ a. I feel uncomfortable.
   - ○ b. I can usually find something to talk about.
   - ○ c. I ask a lot of questions.

2. **When I go to a store or a restaurant, the server or salesperson …**
   - ○ a. usually serves me quickly.
   - ○ b. often ignores me or keeps me waiting.
   - ○ c. is often rude to me.

3. **When I am sitting, I usually …**
   - ○ a. sit up straight.
   - ○ b. do not sit up straight.
   - ○ c. take up a lot of space.

4. **When I need to get someone's attention, I …**
   - ○ a. speak loudly or shout.
   - ○ b. say, "Excuse me" first.
   - ○ c. tap the person on the arm or shoulder.

5. **My friends and family talk to me about my manners …**
   - ○ a. often.
   - ○ b. sometimes.
   - ○ c. never.

6. **I usually speak …**
   - ○ a. a little more formally than most people.
   - ○ b. about the same as other people.
   - ○ c. less formally than other people.

7. **When I meet someone for the first time, …**
   - ○ a. I do most of the talking.
   - ○ b. I talk about half the time and listen half the time.
   - ○ c. I listen and let the other person talk.

8. **When people first meet me, they often think I am …**
   - ○ a. very serious.
   - ○ b. shy and a little nervous.
   - ○ c. outgoing and friendly.
   - ○ d. other _____.

D Look at your answers. Do you think you make a good first impression? Discuss your answers with a partner.

READING 1 | How to Make a Strong First Impression

VOCABULARY

Here are some words from Reading 1. Read the sentences. Then match each bold word with its definition below.

___f___ 1. The child was afraid of the **stranger**. He feels more comfortable with people he knows.

_____ 2. Our cooking teacher likes to **demonstrate** new things before we try them ourselves. Last week, he showed us how to make potato soup.

_____ 3. People with **confidence** usually make better public speakers because they feel very comfortable standing in front of a lot of people.

_____ 4. The academic **standards** at that university are high. It only accepts students with very good grades.

_____ 5. Paris is a city that has a lot of **cultural** attractions for tourists to visit, such as museums and theaters.

_____ 6. You should **select** what you wear to a job interview very carefully. What you wear to an interview is very important.

_____ 7. I really **appreciate** my sister. She always gives me good advice.

_____ 8. Andrew wanted to **impress** the interviewer, so he told her about the important project he worked on.

_____ 9. To **maintain** your health, you should eat well and exercise.

_____ 10. When you travel to other countries, you should learn about the culture first so you don't do or say anything **offensive** to people.

a. (*adj.*) connected with art, music, or literature
b. (*n.*) the feeling that you are sure about your own beliefs or abilities
c. (*v.*) to make someone admire and respect you
d. (*n.*) a level of quality that you use to compare things
e. (*v.*) to choose someone or something from similar people or things
f. (*n.*) a person you do not know
g. (*v.*) to enjoy or to understand the value of someone or something
h. (*adj.*) unpleasant or insulting
i. (*v.*) to show or explain how to do something
j. (*v.*) to continue to have something; to keep something at the same level

PREVIEW READING 1

This is a magazine article. It gives advice on how to make a good first impression. Read the title and headings. What ideas do you think the article will suggest as ways to get other people to like you?

Check (✓) your prediction.

☐ show people you are interested in them

☐ try to impress other people with your stories

 CD 1
Track 3 **Read the article.**

How to Make a Strong First Impression

1   You've heard it before: You only have one chance to make a first impression. According to research, we have about ten seconds with **strangers** before they form an opinion of us.

Body Language and Appearance

2   **Demonstrate** a good attitude with your body. When you first walk into a room, show **confidence**. Stand up straight and look other people in the eye. If you smile frequently, it will make other people more comfortable. They will think you are friendly.

3   Appearance is important. Several years ago, a professional colleague offered to meet

me for lunch. I wore a sport coat and tie. He showed up in shorts and sandals. The message I received was: "Bill, meeting you is a rather ordinary experience. I don't need to present a businesslike appearance." Not surprisingly, that was the last time I met with him. True, **standards** for appropriate clothing have changed a lot. Maybe the best advice I can share came from someone I met. She said, "I don't dress for the job I have now; I dress for the job I want to have."

Voice

4   The way you speak also affects the first impression you make. Listeners judge our intelligence, our level of **cultural** knowledge, even our leadership ability by the words we **select**—and by how we say them. Your listeners hear your tone of voice before they begin listening to your words. Speak clearly and loudly enough so that people can hear you. Change the pitch of your voice to avoid a dull monotone[1]. Show expression in both your voice and your face. And try not to speak too quickly.

Conversation Skills

5   The greatest way to make a good first impression is to demonstrate that the other

---

[1] **monotone:** a way of speaking in which the tone and volume remain the same

person, not you, is the center of attention. When you are only interested in talking about yourself, other people don't feel that you **appreciate** them. Show that you are interested in others. Then new acquaintances will want to see you again. Recently I went to a conference. At lunch, my wife and I sat with several people we didn't know. While most of the people made good impressions, one man did not. He talked about himself the entire time. No one else got a chance to speak. Unfortunately, he probably thought we were interested in his life story. We decided to avoid him all weekend. I like this definition of a bore: "Somebody who talks about himself so much that you don't get to talk about yourself."

6   You'll **impress** other people when you practice good listening skills. Give interested responses: "Hmmm ... interesting!" "Tell me more, please." "What did you do next?" Your partner will welcome your help in keeping the conversation going. You also show you're a good listener when you **maintain** steady eye contact. Think about how you feel when someone you are talking to looks around the room. You think the person would rather be talking to someone else. Try to use the name of the person you've just met frequently. "Judy, I like that suggestion." "Your vacation must have been exciting, Fred." You show that you have paid attention from the start, catching the name during the introduction. Equally important, you'll make conversations more personal by including the listener's name several times.

7   Finally, avoid making other people uncomfortable. Be careful with jokes. Something you think is funny may be **offensive** to others. You don't want to hurt someone's feelings. Also, don't disagree with someone you have just met. If you disagree too much in your first conversation, the other person may think you are just too different. When you know the person better, you can express another opinion.

MAIN IDEAS

Read the statements. Write *T* (true) or *F* (false), according to the reading.

_T_ 1. Appearance is important in making first impressions.

____ 2. You should speak in a soft voice.

____ 3. People will like you better if you show interest in them.

____ 4. You should ask questions and make comments to show you are listening.

____ 5. It's a good idea to tell a few jokes when you meet someone for the first time.

DETAILS

Answer these questions.

1. What are some ways you can make a good impression with your body language?

   _____

2. If you wear very casual clothing to a meeting, what message do you give?

   _____

3. How does the way you speak affect a listener's impression of you?

   _____

4. Why should you maintain eye contact with people when you talk with them?

   _____

5. What is one way to show you are paying attention?

   _____

6. Why should you avoid disagreeing with people you have just met?

   _____

 ## WHAT DO YOU THINK?

Discuss the questions in a group. Then choose one question and write five to eight sentences in response.

Tip) Critical Thinking

In What Do You Think?, you are asked to choose one question and write five to eight sentences. This means you have to **explain** your ideas. When you explain, you give a more complete answer and provide enough information so others can understand. **Explaining** ideas helps you understand and remember information better.

1. Are there any topics of conversation you should avoid when meeting someone for the first time? What are they?

2. Why do you think that people are more interested in themselves than in other people?

3. Do you agree that showing an interest in other people is the best way to make a good first impression? What other ways are there to make a good first impression?

A paragraph is a group of sentences about the same topic. The **main idea** is usually given in the first sentence. This is called the **topic sentence**. The other sentences add details about the topic. They are called supporting sentences and contain **supporting details**, such as examples, explanations, facts, definitions, and reasons.

Identifying main ideas and supporting details is an important skill that will help you become a more effective reader. When you read, skim for main ideas and scan for details.

A. Read the sentences from Reading 1. Write *MI* for the main idea of the paragraph. Write *SD* for the supporting details.

1. Paragraph 4

   ____ a. Speak clearly and loudly enough so that people can hear you.

   ____ b. The way you speak also affects the first impression you make.

   ____ c. And try not to speak too quickly.

2. Paragraph 5

   ____ a. He talked about himself the entire time.

   ____ b. When you are only interested in talking about yourself, other people don't feel that you appreciate them.

   ____ c. The greatest way to make a good first impression is to demonstrate that the other person, not you, is the center of attention.

3. Paragraph 6

   ____ a. You'll impress other people when you practice good listening skills.

   ____ b. Give interested responses.

   ____ c. You also show you're a good listener when you maintain steady eye contact.

B. Look again at Paragraphs 2, 3, and 7 in Reading 1. Underline the topic sentence that states each paragraph's main idea. Then compare your answers with a partner.

Job Interviews 101

VOCABULARY

Here are some words from Reading 2. Read their definitions. Then complete each sentence.

> **accomplishment** (*n.*) something impressive that someone has achieved
> **consider** (*v.*) to have something as your opinion; to think about someone or something in a particular way
> **exaggerate** (*v.*) to make something seem larger, better, or worse than it really is
> **expect** (*v.*) to think or believe that someone will do something or something will happen
> **professional** (*adj.*) doing something in a way that shows skill, training, and care
> **punctual** (*adj.*) doing something or happening at the right time; not late
> **research** (*n.*) a detailed and careful study of something to find out more about it
> **responsible** (*adj.*) behaving well and in a sensible way
> **slang** (*n.*) informal words and expressions that are more common in spoken language
> **weakness** (*n.*) a fault or lack of strength, especially in a person's character

1. When you speak to customers, you should always be _____.
   You should be polite and try to help them as quickly as you can.

2. Stan's greatest _____ is junk food. He eats fast food for
   almost every meal!

3. You were late for work again today. I _____ you to arrive on
   time tomorrow.

4. Mehmet is always _____. He's never late for anything.

5. Takeshi is very _____. He always pays his bills on time and
   never does anything he knows is dangerous.

6. Many teenagers use so much _____ when they talk to each
   other that their own parents can't understand them.

7. You are not allowed to use your cell phone in some restaurants now
   because many people _____ it rude.

8. My grandfather did a lot of interesting things during his life, but his
   greatest _____ was climbing Mount Everest.

9. Scott likes to _____ when he tells a story. Yesterday, he told us he caught a fish that weighed 20 pounds, but it really only weighed 5 pounds.

10. Scientists are doing _____ to find out about the possible health benefits of green tea.

PREVIEW READING 2

This is an article from a career magazine. It discusses what to do and what not to do during a job interview. Read the title and the first sentence in each paragraph.

Check (✓) all the things you think the article will say you should do at a job interview.

☐ a. Find out as much as you can about the job.
☐ b. Wear your most comfortable clothing.
☐ c. Don't smile; you want the interviewer to take you seriously.
☐ d. Let the interviewer do all the talking.
☐ e. Interrupt the interviewer when you have something important to say.

 CD 1 Track 4 **Read the article.**

Job Interviews 101

1   You finally got that call you have been waiting for—an interview for a new job. At first, you will probably feel overjoyed[1], but as the interview gets closer, you are likely to get more and more nervous about the big day. Experts say that you only have 30 seconds to make a good first impression at a job interview. The key to a successful interview is to be prepared and stay **professional** at all times. To make sure you do your best, remember these ten tips:

2   *Be prepared.* Learn as much as you can about the company before the interview. Go to the business's website and read it so you are aware of how things work there. Think of questions the interviewer might ask you and practice your answers with a friend. Know how to discuss both your strengths and your **weaknesses** because you will be asked about both!

¹ **overjoyed:** very happy

3   *Dress the part.* If you walk in wearing jeans and a T-shirt, you are not likely to get the position. Wear clothing that is neat, clean, and presentable. Most companies **expect** applicants to wear business clothes, such as a shirt and tie or a nice suit. Dressing well shows that you are serious about the job.

4   *Be **punctual**.* Arriving late to an interview can be deadly. No employer wants to hire someone who is not **responsible** enough to come to work on time. Get to the interview 10–15 minutes early to help yourself relax before you step into the office.

5   *Make eye contact.* Look your interviewer in the eye when you greet him or her and keep eye contact throughout the entire interview. Keeping eye contact shows the other person that you are both honest and confident.

6   *Be polite.* Sit up straight when you are being interviewed, listen carefully to what the interviewer is saying, and avoid using **slang** or bad words. If you don't understand a question, ask politely, "Could you please repeat that?" When you are polite, you appear more professional and are more likely to get the job.

7   *Don't interrupt[2].* Interrupting is **considered** rude. Let the interviewer finish what she or he is saying. If you have something important to say, try to remember it and wait for a moment of silence to speak up.

8   *Find shared interests.* Try to notice what the interviewer finds important. Listen for topics that you both know something about and discuss them. If you can't think of anything, nod[3] yes or agree with points that the interviewer makes.

9   *Sell yourself.* Don't be afraid to talk about your **accomplishments**. Employers want to hire people who are successful and confident in their abilities. However, be careful not to **exaggerate**. Do not lie about past job responsibilities. You don't want employers to ask your old boss about things you never did!

10   *Stay positive.* Avoid complaining about a bad boss or job you had before. Being negative can make employers worry that you are not a team player, or that you don't work well with others. And remember to smile. Smiling shows you are easygoing and enthusiastic.

11   *Ask questions.* At the end of the interview, ask specific questions about the job or company, such as "What kind of work can I expect to be doing the first year?" or "Where do you see the company five years from now?" You want to show the employer that you have done your **research** and that you care about working there.

12   Interviewing is not easy, but it is easier when you know what to do and what to expect. If you stay honest and professional, you will get yourself one step closer to the job you want. Oh, and one more thing: don't forget to breathe!

---

[2] **interrupt:** to make somebody stop speaking

[3] **nod:** to move your head down and then up again quickly as a way of saying yes

MAIN IDEAS

Complete the T-chart with *Dos* and *Don'ts* of job interviewing, according to the article.

Job Interview *Dos*	Job Interview *Don'ts*
Dress professionally.	Don't be negative.

DETAILS

Read the statements. Write *T* (true) or *F* (false). Then correct each false statement to make it true according to the article.

_____ 1. Learn as much as you can about the company before the interview.

_____ 2. Most companies expect applicants to wear casual clothes to an interview.

_____ 3. Get to the interview 30–40 minutes early so you can start the interview early.

_____ 4. Keeping eye contact shows the interviewer that you are a good listener.

_____ 5. It's OK to lie a little bit about a past job in order to impress your interviewer.

_____ 6. Avoid complaining about a good or bad boss you had before.

_____ 7. At the end of the interview, tell the interviewer a personal story.

WHAT DO YOU THINK?

A. Discuss the questions in a group. Then choose one question and write five to eight sentences in response.

1. Which job interview tip from Reading 2 do you think is the most important? Which is the hardest to do? Why?

2. In your opinion, what is the best way to make a job interviewer interested in you?

B. Think about both Reading 1 and Reading 2 as you discuss the questions.

1. What are the best ways to make a good impression on others?

2. What are the best ways to avoid making a bad impression on others?

3. Can you make a good first impression the same way in every situation (e.g., at a job interview, talking to a customer, meeting a new classmate, etc.)? Why or why not?

Vocabulary Skill | **Using the dictionary**

Word Forms

Learning word forms increases your vocabulary. It will help make your reading, speaking, and writing more fluent. Look at the dictionary definitions below.

ac·com·plish /əˈkɑmplɪʃ/ *verb* [T] to succeed in doing something difficult that you planned to do: *Very little was accomplished at the meeting.* **SYN** **achieve**

ac·com·plished /əˈkɑmplɪʃt/ *adj.* highly skilled at something: *an accomplished pianist*

ac·com·plish·ment /əˈkɑmplɪʃmənt/ *noun* **1** [C] something difficult that someone has succeeded in doing or learning: *He was proud of his academic accomplishments.* **2** (*formal*) [U] the act of completing something successfully

All dictionary entries are from the *Oxford American Dictionary for learners of English* © Oxford University Press 2011.

A. Complete the chart. An *X* indicates that a word form doesn't exist or you don't need to know it at this time. Use your dictionary to help you.

	Noun	Verb	Adjective	Adverb
1.	accomplishment	*accomplish*	*accomplished*	X
2.			considerable	considerably
3.	confidence	X		
4.		demonstrate		X
5.		impress		X
6.		offend		
7.		X	responsible	
8.		select		

Tip for Success

Many words have the same noun and verb form. For example, *tie* can be a noun or a verb.

B. Complete each sentence with a word from Activity A. Choose a word from the row in the chart indicated in parentheses.

1. My biggest (1) __accomplishment__ in life so far has been my graduation from high school.

2. Appearance is an important (2) _____ if you want to make a good impression. Think carefully about how you will look to others.

3. When you speak in public, you need to show (3) _____. Even if you are nervous, you should look as if you are not.

4. Keeping eye contact will (4) _____ to others that you are interested in what they are saying.

5. The person who applied for the job had a(n) (5) _____ work history. The manager was surprised at the high-level positions she had held in her previous jobs.

6. Don't tell jokes when you meet people for the first time because you might (6) _____ them and make them angry or upset.

C. Choose two sets of words from Activity A. Write one sentence for each form of the word in your notebook. Then share your sentences with a partner.

WRITING

Developing a paragraph

A paragraph should discuss one main idea from beginning to end and develop the main idea with specific details.

- The **topic sentence** is usually the first sentence of a paragraph. It identifies the topic, or subject, of the paragraph. It also gives the main idea (or controlling idea), which explains what the writer will say about the topic.
- The **supporting sentences** are the middle sentences of a paragraph. They support the topic sentence with two or three smaller ideas, or subtopics. Subtopics are supported with specific details, such as examples, explanations, facts, definitions, and reasons.
- The **concluding sentence** is usually the last sentence of a paragraph. It summarizes the main points of the paragraph and restates the topic sentence, but in different words.

A. Read the paragraph.

When you start a job, you can leave a bad impression on your new co-workers very quickly without even realizing it. Because the workplace can be fast-paced and stressful, it can be easy to forget the people around you. One sure way to annoy your co-workers is to speak loudly on your phone. Speaking loudly on the phone can make it difficult for your co-workers to focus on what they are doing or to have phone conversations of their own. It may also send a message that you think your work and phone conversations are more important than anyone else's. Another common mistake is to take the last cup of coffee and not make another pot. Leaving an empty coffee pot means that the next person has to take the time to make a new pot of coffee. Nobody likes to do this, particularly first thing in the morning! Many people find this behavior very rude. Leaving your cell phone on is another way you could unknowingly irritate your co-workers and cause them to form a bad impression of you. Your ringing cell phone may disturb the quiet your co-workers need to do their work. The noise may cause them to work more slowly or make mistakes. Also, many people consider it disrespectful. Finding your dream job may take a lot of time and effort, but unfortunately, leaving a bad impression on your co-workers can be done quickly and easily!

B. Circle the topic sentence of the paragraph in Activity A.

C. Underline the supporting sentences in the paragraph. Circle the concluding sentence. Then compare your answers with a partner.

An **outline** is a plan you make before you start writing. Outlines help you put your ideas in order. When you write an outline for a paragraph, include the topic sentence, the subtopics, important supporting details, and the concluding sentence.

Example of an outline

1. **Topic sentence:** When you start a job, you can leave a bad impression on your new co-workers very quickly without even realizing it.
2. **Subtopics and supporting details:**
   A. talking loudly on your phone
      1. co-workers can't focus or have phone calls
      2. sends a message
   B. taking the last cup of coffee
      1. someone else has to make more
      2. many people find it rude
   C. leaving cell phone on
      1. co-workers may work more slowly or make mistakes
      2. many people consider it disrespectful
3. **Concluding sentence:** Finding your dream job may take a lot of time and effort, but unfortunately, leaving a bad impression on your co-workers can be done quickly and easily!

Read the paragraph. Then complete the outline on page 18.

Fixing a Negative Impression

Sometimes we say something that leaves people with a bad impression, but it is possible to fix the situation. First, you must figure out why you have made others upset or uninterested. Think about the conversation you had earlier and try to remember what you said that offended others. For example, sometimes we tell a joke that they do not think is funny. Second, be prepared for the next time you see them. Make a plan about what you want to say and what topics you should avoid. You do not want to make the same mistake twice! Finally, when you see them again, be positive and act interested. Do not bring up the bad past experience. Instead, focus on the present. You should get them to talk a lot so that they feel more comfortable around you. Ask them questions, listen carefully to their answers, and respond with thoughtful comments that show you care about what they have to say. There is no magic formula to turn a negative impression into a positive one; however, if you stay positive and seem interested in changing their opinion about you, you are more likely to get them to like you the next time!

1. Topic sentence: <u>Sometimes we say something that leaves people with a</u>

   <u>bad impression, but it is possible to fix the situation.</u>

2. Subtopics and supporting details:

   A. _____

      1. <u>Think about the conversation.</u>

      2. _____

   B. <u>Be prepared.</u>

      1. _____

      2. _____

   C. _____

      1. <u>Don't bring up the bad past experience.</u>

      2. _____

3. Concluding sentence: _____

   _____

Grammar | Real conditionals: present and future

The **present real conditional** is used to talk about general truths, habits, and things that happen again and again. It is formed by using the simple present in both the *if* clause (the condition) and the result clause.

if clause	result clause

If you **walk** in wearing jeans and a T-shirt, you **are not likely** to get the position.

You can also use a modal (*may, might, would, could*) in the result clause.

if clause	result clause

If you **disagree** too much in your first conversation, the other person **may think**

you are just too different.

The **future real conditional** is used to talk about what will happen under certain conditions. The *if* clause gives the condition. The result clause gives the result. The future real conditional is formed by using the simple present in the *if* clause and the future with *will* or *be going to* in the result clause.

if clause	result clause

If you **smile** frequently, it **will make** other people more comfortable.

	if clause		result clause	

If you **stay** honest and professional, you **will get** one step closer to the job you want.

You can also use *when* or *whenever* instead of *if* for both the present real conditional and future real conditional.

	when clause		result clause	

When you **take care of** yourself, you **feel** better!

	result clause		*when* clause	

You**'ll impress** other people when you **practice** good listening skills.

	when clause		result clause	

When you **are interested** in other people, they **will** probably **be interested** in you.

A. Underline the *if* or *when* clause and circle the result clause.

1. People want to be around you when you have good listening skills.

2. If you tell a joke, you could offend someone.

3. When you dress appropriately, people take you seriously.

4. You are more likely to make a good impression if you are confident and prepared.

5. If you don't ask questions, people may not think you're interested in what they're saying.

B. Complete each sentence with the correct form of the verb in parentheses. There may be more than one correct answer.

1. If they offer me the job, I think I _____will take_____ it. (take)

2. I _____ better when I exercise regularly. (feel)

3. If a student pays attention in class, the teacher _____ a good first impression of her or him. (have)

4. If you _____ unprepared, the interviewer might think you are not serious. (come)

5. He probably won't pass if he _____. (not, study)

C. Complete each sentence with your own ideas.

1. If I don't get enough sleep, _____.

2. If you don't prepare for the interview, _____.

3. If you don't pay attention to your friend, _____.

4. If you tell a joke, _____.

5. If you arrive 15 minutes late to a job interview, _____

_____.

Unit Assignment | **Write a "how to" paragraph**

 In this assignment, you are going to organize, develop, and write a "how to" paragraph. As you prepare your paragraph, think about the Unit Question, "How do you make a good first impression?" Refer to the Self-Assessment checklist on page 22. Use information from Readings 1 and 2 and your work in this unit to support your ideas.

For alternative unit assignments, see the *Q: Skills for Success Teacher's Handbook.*

PLAN AND WRITE

A. **BRAINSTORM** Follow these steps to choose a topic and to brainstorm ideas about your topic.

1. Look at the topics and add your own idea. Then choose one of the topics to write about.

How to make a good first impression on:	
a classmate	a college roommate
a teacher	a friend's parents
a new neighbor	your idea: _____

 **Your Writing Process**

For this activity, you could also use Stage 1A, *Freewriting* in *Q Online Practice*.

2. Think about your topic and write it below. Brainstorm some things you should do or should not do to make a good first impression. Make a list of do's and don'ts in the T-chart.

My topic: _____

Dos	Don'ts

B. **PLAN** Write an outline for your paragraph. Look back at the Writing Skill on page 17 to help you.

1. Topic sentence: _____

_____

_____

2. Subtopics and supporting details:

   A. _____

      _____

      1. _____

      2. _____

   B. _____

      _____

      1. _____

      2. _____

C. _____

_____

    1. _____

    2. _____

3. **Concluding sentence:** _____

_____

_____

C. WRITE Use your outline from Activity B to help you write your paragraph in your notebook. Look at the Self-Assessment checklist below to guide your writing.

REVISE AND EDIT

A. PEER REVIEW Read a partner's paragraph. Answer the questions and discuss them with your partner.

1. Does the paragraph answer the Unit Question?

2. Is there a clear topic sentence? Is there a concluding sentence? Underline them.

3. Are there enough details to support the topic sentence?

4. Do you think someone would make a good first impression if he or she followed the suggestions in the paragraph?

B. REWRITE Review the answers to the questions in Activity A. You may want to revise and rewrite your paragraph.

C. EDIT Complete the Self-Assessment checklist as you prepare to write the final draft of your paragraph. Be prepared to hand in your work or discuss it in class.

SELF-ASSESSMENT		
Yes	No	
☐	☐	Is the punctuation correct?
☐	☐	Are all words spelled correctly?
☐	☐	Does the paragraph include vocabulary from the unit?
☐	☐	Are all words used in their correct form?
☐	☐	Does the paragraph include conditionals? Are they used correctly?

Circle the words you learned in this unit.

Nouns
accomplishment
confidence 🔑
research 🔑 AWL
slang
standard 🔑
stranger 🔑
weakness 🔑

Verbs
appreciate 🔑 AWL
consider 🔑
demonstrate 🔑 AWL
exaggerate 🔑
expect 🔑
impress 🔑
maintain 🔑 AWL
select 🔑 AWL

Adjectives
cultural 🔑 AWL
offensive 🔑
professional 🔑 AWL
punctual
responsible 🔑

🔑 Oxford 3000™ words
AWL Academic Word List
For more information on the Oxford 3000™ and the AWL, see page xi.

Check (✓) the skills you learned. If you need more work on a skill, refer to the page(s) in parentheses.

READING	●	I can identify main ideas and supporting details. (p. 9)
VOCABULARY	●	I can use the dictionary to find word forms. (p. 14)
WRITING	●	I can organize and develop a paragraph. (pp. 16–17)
GRAMMAR	●	I can use real conditionals. (pp. 18–19)
LEARNING OUTCOME	●	I can develop a "how to" paragraph that details the steps involved in making a good impression.

UNIT 2

Food and Taste

READING ● previewing a text
VOCABULARY ● use of context to understand words
WRITING ● using descriptive adjectives
GRAMMAR ● use and placement of adjectives

LEARNING OUTCOME

Write a paragraph about your favorite dish using descriptive adjectives.

Unit QUESTION

What makes food taste good?

PREVIEW THE UNIT

A Discuss these questions with your classmates.

What kinds of foods do you eat every day?

What foods do you have on special occasions, such as holidays or birthdays?

Look at the photo. Do you think how food looks—its presentation—affects how it tastes? Explain.

B Discuss the Unit Question above with your classmates.

Listen to *The Q Classroom*, Track 5 on CD 1, to hear other answers.

C Take the quiz to discover what tastes you prefer. Circle your answers.

WHAT
TASTES
DO YOU PREFER?

1. **What kind of juice do you prefer?**
   a. pineapple
   b. orange
   c. grapefruit

2. **When eating at a restaurant, do you prefer to have an appetizer or a dessert?**
   a. appetizer
   b. dessert
   c. both

3. **For a snack, which do you prefer?**
   a. crackers and cheese
   b. cookies
   c. carrots

4. **Do you drink coffee or tea? If so, how do you like it?**
   a. black (no milk or sugar)
   b. with milk
   c. with sugar
   d. with milk and sugar

5. **Which do you prefer to have for dessert?**
   a. vanilla ice cream
   b. chocolate cake
   c. I don't like sweets.

D Work with a partner. Discuss your answers to the questions in Activity C. Then answer the questions below.

1. Foods can have different tastes. They include sweet, sour, salty, and bitter. What did your answers tell you about the types of foods you prefer?

2. Were your answers very different from your partner's answers? If so, what is one way to explain the differences?

READING

VOCABULARY

Here are some words and phrases from Reading 1. Read their definitions. Then complete each sentence. Compare your answers with a partner.

> **balanced** (*adj.*) consisting of parts that are in the correct or pleasing proportions
>
> **identify** (*v.*) to recognize or be able to say who or what something is
>
> **likely** (*adj.*) probable or expected
>
> **be made up of** (*phr.*) to consist of
>
> **at risk** (*phr.*) in danger
>
> **recognize** (*v.*) to know again someone or something that you have seen or heard before
>
> **sensitive** (*adj.*) easily hurt or damaged by something
>
> **system** (*n.*) a group of things or parts that work together
>
> **typically** (*adv.*) usually, normally

1. I did not _____ Rosa at first because she had a new short haircut. She had very long hair the last time I saw her.

2. Water _____ hydrogen and oxygen.

3. The human digestive _____ includes the mouth and stomach. It helps to change the food we eat into energy.

4. People who don't eat well are more _____ to get sick than people with healthy diets.

5. People who eat healthy foods and exercise _____ have fewer health problems than people who don't.

6. Su-jeong is very _____ to cold, so she usually wears a scarf and a sweater, even in warm weather.

7. Most health experts agree that a _____ diet should include different types of foods, such as meat, fruits, vegetables, bread, and cheese.

8. People who don't sleep enough are _____ of getting sick. When you're tired, it's much easier to catch a cold or the flu.

9. The police used a photograph to _____ the man who stole Anita's wallet.

PREVIEW READING 1

This is a magazine article. It discusses taste and why people like and dislike certain foods. Look at the photos and subheadings. Why do you think people like and dislike certain foods?

What do you already know about this topic?

CD 1
Track 6 Read the article.

Knowing Your Tastes

Food Likes and Dislikes

1   Why do some people love spicy food and others hate it? Why do many people dislike broccoli? Why do some people want sweets all the time? Human taste is not as simple as liking or disliking something. The kind of tongue you have can affect your food choices—and your health.

How the Tongue Works

2   The human tongue **is made up of** a group of muscles and taste buds that work together to **recognize** taste. The average adult tongue has 10,000 taste buds, which are tiny bumps located on the tongue. Tiny hairs on the end of the taste buds tell us whether food is sweet, sour, bitter, or salty. The taste buds send messages to the brain as chemicals from the food enter the nose. Together, the taste buds and nose tell the brain exactly what the tongue is tasting. This complex **system** helps humans survive by recognizing which foods are safe and which might be dangerous.

Nontasters, Medium Tasters, Supertasters

3   Although all humans have taste buds, we do not all have the same number of them.

Medium tasters **typically** have 10,000 taste buds. These "average tasters" make up about 50 percent of the world population. *Nontasters*, 25 percent of the population, have half the number of taste buds as medium tasters. The remaining 25 percent are *supertasters*. Supertasters have four to six times as many taste buds as nontasters and twice as many as medium tasters (see Figure 1). Research shows that supertasters are more **likely** to be women and from Asia, Africa, and South America.

Different Worlds for Different Tasters

4   Supertasters live in a very colorful world of tastes, nontasters live in a gray world, and medium tasters are somewhere between the two. Supertasters think that a lot of foods are too strong. In addition to having more taste buds, supertasters are born with a gene[1] that makes them **sensitive** to bitter foods. Consequently, they dislike broccoli, cauliflower, grapefruit, and even coffee. With more taste buds, they can more easily feel fatty foods in their mouths. As a result, they stay away from high-fat food items like french fries and sweets. They are also very sensitive

---

[1] **gene:** a part of a cell in a living thing that decides its characteristics

to pain on the tongue, so they avoid spicy food. Nontasters, on the other hand, experience fewer tastes in general, so they can enjoy hot foods like chili and pepper with much less pain.

Supertasters, Nontasters, and Diet

5   As a rule, humans avoid foods that taste bad and eat foods that give them pleasure. Since supertasters avoid bitter fruits and vegetables, their diets are sometimes not **balanced**, which could put them more **at risk** for certain types of cancers. However, they also dislike fatty and sweet foods, so they tend to be thinner and at lower risk for heart disease and diabetes[2]. In contrast, nontasters like foods high in fat because their tongues do not react negatively to them. All people should pay attention to what they eat, but nontasters and supertasters must be more aware of the foods they are consuming or avoiding and find other ways to make up the difference.

What Kind of "Taster" Are You?

6   If you can **identify** which kind of taster you are, you will be able to make more educated choices about your diet. This simple test can show whether you are a nontaster, medium taster, or supertaster. Put a small amount of blue food coloring on your tongue. Take a piece of notebook paper (the kind with three holes punched out), and put one of the holes over your tongue. Your taste buds will look like little pink bumps on your blue tongue. Count how many bumps you see in the hole. If there are five bumps or fewer, you are a nontaster. If there are 30 or more, you are a supertaster. If there are between 5 and 30, you're a medium taster.

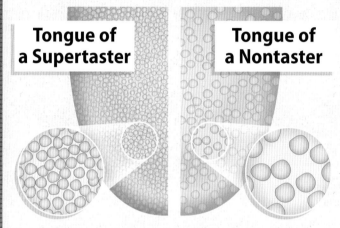

Tongue of a Supertaster

Tongue of a Nontaster

Figure 1 Supertasters have many more taste buds than nontasters.

[2] **diabetes:** a serious disease in which a person's body cannot control the level of sugar in the body

MAIN IDEAS

Circle the answer to each question.

1. What is the main idea of the article?
    a. As a rule, humans eat foods that taste good and avoid foods that taste bad.
    b. The kind of taster you are can affect both your food choices and your health.
    c. Supertasters live in a colorful world of taste, but nontasters live in a gray world.

2. Which statement is true about taste buds?
    a. They tell the brain how food tastes.
    b. They send messages to the tongue.
    c. The average person has 5,000 taste buds.

3. Which statement is true about the number of taste buds a person has?
    a. How many taste buds you have has no effect on taste.
    b. The number of taste buds you have can cause you to like or dislike certain foods.
    c. The more taste buds you have, the more you enjoy spicy foods.

4. Which statement is true about the three different kinds of tasters?
    a. Finding out what kind of taster you are can help you make important decisions about your diet.
    b. Supertasters are more likely to be men from Asia, Africa, and South America.
    c. You need a complex test to show you what kind of taster you are.

DETAILS

Answer these questions. Then compare your answers with a partner.

1. What four tastes can taste buds identify?

   _____

2. How many taste buds do nontasters have?

   _____

3. Who is more likely to be a supertaster, a woman from Italy or a woman from Korea?

   _____

4. What types of foods do supertasters avoid?

   _____

5. Why should supertasters and nontasters pay close attention to the foods they eat?

   _____

WHAT DO YOU THINK?

Discuss the questions in a group. Then choose one question and write five to eight sentences in response.

1. Do you think you are a nontaster, medium taster, or supertaster? Why?

2. What foods do you really like or dislike? Choose one food and describe what you like or dislike about it.

3. In addition to the type of tasters they are, what are other possible reasons why people like certain foods and don't like others?

READING 2 | Finding Balance in Food

VOCABULARY

Here are some words from Reading 2. Cross out the word that is different from the bold word. Then compare your answers with a partner.

1. People who **consume** too many calories typically gain weight.
   a. take in   ~~b. waste~~   c. eat

2. The foods we eat often during childhood can **influence** the foods we prefer as adults.
   a. make   b. affect   c. help determine

3. The **concept** behind organic food is that farmers should grow fruits, vegetables, and grains without harmful chemicals.
   a. idea   b. part   c. belief

4. Normandy, a northern **region** of France, is home to many famous cheeses.
   a. area   b. place   c. direction

5. Italian **cuisine** is known for its rich, fresh sauces and its pasta dishes.
   a. history   b. cooking   c. food

6. I had a very healthy dinner last night. I ate meat, vegetables, some fruit, and just a small **portion** of dessert.
   a. amount   b. kind   c. quantity

7. The **practice** of eating with one's hands is considered rude in some cultures but polite in others.
   a. action   b. advantage   c. custom

8. A unique **property** of water is that it takes up more space when it is ice than when it is a liquid.
    a. quality   b. characteristic   c. size

9. One **principle** of vegetarian diets is that eating fruits, grains, and vegetables is healthier for you than eating a meat-based diet.
    a. basic rule   b. decision   c. belief

10. Various cultures use different **methods** for preparing foods.
    a. problems   b. ways   c. processes

Reading Skill | Previewing a text

Previewing means looking through a text quickly to find the topic and main ideas before you read the whole text. Previewing gives you a general understanding of the reading first, which will help you when you read the whole text from beginning to end. When you preview, the goal is to predict what the text is going to talk about.

Previewing usually includes these steps:
- reading the title and subtitles
- looking at the photographs and pictures
- reading the first and last paragraphs

After you preview a text, you should be able to answer these questions:
- What is the topic of the reading?
- What ideas are discussed in the reading?

A. Look at Reading 2. Follow these steps as you preview the text.

Step 1: Read the title and subtitles.

1. What is the title of the reading? Write it below.

    _____

2. There are four headings within the reading. Write them below:

    _Food, Balance, and Culture_____

    _____

    _____

    _____

Step 2: Look at the pictures.

Look at the photo and pictures. What are they of?

_____

_____

Step 3: Read the first and last paragraphs.

Read the first and last paragraphs quickly. Underline the topic sentence of each paragraph.

B. What is the topic of the reading?

_____

C. What ideas are discussed in the reading?

_____

PREVIEW READING 2

This is an article from an online food magazine that discusses how culture can affect people's food choices. Look back at your answers to the questions in the Reading Skill activities above. What do you already know about this topic?

 CD 1
Track 7

Read the article.

Finding Balance in Food

Food, Balance, and Culture

1   Nutritionists around the world often speak about the importance of a balanced diet. A balanced diet usually means eating more fruits, vegetables, and grains and **consuming** fewer foods high in fat, sugar, and cholesterol. When comparing the food habits of different cultures, however, the definition of a "balanced diet" might also be seen differently. A person's culture can **influence** the way he tries to find balance in the foods he consumes. Cultures might view balance differently according to the way a dish tastes, or how a meal is prepared and served. Looking at the **concept** of a "balanced diet" through the eyes of two very different cultures makes it clear that the definition can differ greatly.

France: Balancing Geography and Portions

2   For the French, balance does not come only from using different kinds of ingredients; enjoying the tastes of the country's many **regions** can also make their diet feel balanced. France is divided into 22 regions.

Figure 1 France has 22 different regions.

Each region has its own local **cuisine** and food traditions, or what the French call *terroir*. The French embrace[1] all 22 regions and the cuisine produced in each. French cafés, restaurants, and food advertisements often refer to[2] the different regions, and to the fact that French people find pleasure in eating foods from different parts of the country in a search for balance.

3   One can also see balance in the way the French serve their food. A traditional French meal can have from three to seven different courses. It might include an appetizer, a main plate, a side plate, a cheese plate, a salad, and a dessert, which makes it a well-balanced dining experience. Each dish is eaten and enjoyed separately, and **portions** are small. This **practice** has even affected the menus of fast-food chains. Many French people dislike the traditional fast-food meal because it is too simple and quick, so fast-food restaurants in France have changed their menus. Some now include an appetizer, a main dish, a dessert, and a coffee to offer diners the balance they want.

China: Balancing Yin and Yang

4   Like French cuisine, traditional Chinese cooking also tries to find balance, but in a different way. In China, the concepts of *yin* and *yang* influence the way food is traditionally prepared and eaten by the Chinese. Yin and yang symbolize balance and harmony between opposing forces (Figure 2). According to traditional beliefs, some foods, like carrots, water, and tofu, have yin **properties** because they are "cool" foods, which decrease body heat. In contrast, yang foods, such as chicken, eggs, and mushrooms, are "warm" foods, which increase body heat. The **principles** of yin and yang can apply to cooking **methods** as well. Water-based cooking like boiling and steaming has yin qualities. Frying and roasting are yang methods.

5   The challenge in traditional Chinese cooking is to prepare and eat meals that balance yin and yang qualities. The Chinese believe that

Figure 2 The yin-yang symbol

achieving this kind of balance can result in improved health. For instance, dishes like beef with broccoli and sweet and sour chicken are considered healthy because they have a balance of foods, colors, flavors, and textures. They believe diseases result when there is too much yin or yang in the human body. To the Chinese, food acts as medicine. A person with heartburn might have too much yang because she is eating too much spicy food. As a result, a doctor might tell her to drink iced tea, a source of yin, to balance the yang force.

---

[1] **embrace:** to accept something
[2] **refer to:** to talk about

Different Cultures, Shared Desire

6   France and China have very different cultures, and people in each culture have their own ideas of what constitutes a balanced meal, whether it is tastes, menus, ingredients, eating habits, or nutritional benefits. What connects the two, however, is a shared desire to find some kind of balance. A look at their food preferences also suggests that culture and food are not separate from each other. They are closely related, and their connection can be observed around the world in very different and fascinating ways.

MAIN IDEAS

Circle the answer to each question.

1. What is the main purpose of the article?
    a. to compare how two cultures find balance in food
    b. to explain why the French do not like fast food
    c. to describe the concepts of *yin* and *yang*

2. What is the main idea of Paragraph 2?
    a. Each of the 22 regions in France has its own *terroir*.
    b. In France, balance comes from eating foods from different regions.
    c. The French find pleasure in eating at different kinds of restaurants.

3. What is the main idea of Paragraph 3?
    a. Many French people do not like to eat at fast-food restaurants.
    b. The French balance their meals by serving many small courses.
    c. Some fast-food restaurants in France offer three-course meals.

4. What is the main idea of Paragraph 4?
    a. Yin and yang help create balance in Chinese cooking.
    b. Yang foods are believed to increase body heat.
    c. Carrots and water are yin foods because they are cool.

5. What is the main idea of Paragraph 5?
    a. Preparing balanced meals is a challenge.
    b. Too much yang can cause heartburn.
    c. Meals that balance yin and yang can improve health.

DETAILS

Read the statements. Write _T_ (true) or _F_ (false). Then correct each false statement to make it true.

_____ 1. *Terroir* means local food and traditions.

_____ 2. There are no fast-food restaurants in France.

_____ 3. French meals always have seven courses.

_____ 4. The French prefer to eat small portions of food.

_____ 5. Eggs and mushrooms are considered *yin* foods.

_____ 6. Frying and roasting are *yang* cooking methods.

 WHAT DO YOU THINK?

A. Discuss the questions in a group. Then choose one question and write five to eight sentences in response.

1. Do you prefer to eat more variety but smaller portions of food, or less variety but bigger portions? Why?

2. What foods do you enjoy from cultures other than your own? How are they different from the food you grew up with?

B. Think about both Reading 1 and Reading 2 as you discuss the questions.

1. What makes food taste good to you?

2. Which foods did you dislike as a child? Which foods do you dislike as an adult? Why do you think food preferences change as you get older?

Learning to read without stopping to look up new words can help you read faster and understand more. When reading, try to guess the meaning of a new word from **context**. Context refers to the other words and ideas in the sentence that are around the new word:

> A balanced diet usually means eating more fruits, vegetables, and grains and **consuming** fewer foods high in fat, sugar, and cholesterol.

The context around the word *consuming* suggests that the sentence is about what kinds of food to eat and not eat in order to have a balanced diet. Therefore, you can guess that *consuming* has a similar meaning to *eating*.

If you need to know what a word means, start by guessing from the context. If a sentence does not give enough context, then look the word up in the dictionary.

A. Read each sentence and try to answer the question that follows. (The underlined words are for Activity B.)

1. People in every culture have their own ideas of what <u>constitutes</u> a balanced meal, whether it is tastes, menus, ingredients, eating habits, or nutritional benefits.

   What things can make a balanced meal?

   tastes, menus, ingredients, eating habits, and nutritional benefits

2. Beef with broccoli and sweet and sour chicken are two famous <u>dishes</u> that can be found in most Chinese restaurants.

   What foods are common in Chinese restaurants?

   _____

3. French cheeses can have different <u>textures</u>, from soft cheeses like *Brie* to hard cheeses like *Cantal*.

   In what way can French cheeses differ?

   _____

4. Nontasters have a <u>taste</u> for sugary foods, which means they eat sweets more often than other people.

   Why do nontasters eat sweets?

   _____

5. Cultures might <u>view</u> balance differently according to the way a dish tastes, or how a meal is prepared and served.

In what ways can cultures find balance in food?

_____

6. In traditional Chinese cooking, foods are in <u>harmony</u> when there is an equal amount of *yin* and *yang* foods together.

What foods work together in Chinese cooking?

_____

B. Check (✓) the word or phrase that is closest in meaning to each underlined word from Activity A. Look at the context to help you choose the best word or expression.

1. constitutes

____ a. eats

____ b. makes

2. dishes

____ a. meals

____ b. tastes

3. textures

____ a. ways that things feel

____ b. ways that things smell

4. taste

____ a. an idea

____ b. a liking

5. view

____ a. think about

____ b. eliminate

6. harmony

____ a. a good recipe

____ b. a good combination

C. Choose four words from Activities A and B. Write a sentence using each word.

1. _____

2. _____

3. _____

4. _____

WRITING

Adjectives are words that describe nouns (*people*, *places*, *things*, and *ideas*). Writers use a lot of adjectives in order to make their descriptions both interesting and clear. They describe what they *see*, *hear*, *smell*, *taste*, *touch*, and *feel*. They paint a picture with words so that readers can easily imagine or "see" what they are describing. Using **descriptive adjectives** in your writing will make it more interesting for the reader.

Non-descriptive: I ate a meal at a restaurant downtown.

Descriptive: I ate a **delicious**, **savory** meal at a **cozy French** restaurant downtown.

A. Read the paragraph. Then answer the questions with a partner.

My Mother's Yorkshire Pudding

Whenever I think of my mother's cooking, I always remember her delicious Yorkshire puddings. Although I grew up in the United States, my mother often cooked dishes from her home country of England. She has always been an excellent cook, and one of her best recipes is called Yorkshire pudding, which is a traditional English pastry. It is a simple dish made with eggs, flour, and milk. My mother's Yorkshire puddings taste so good because they are light, crisp, and slightly sweet. She serves them with delicious warm gravy, but I prefer them sweet with strawberry jam. They are very special because she only serves them on holidays. My sister and I always fight for the last one because they are so delicious. I have had many other people's Yorkshire puddings, but my mother's have always tasted better. Not only are hers homemade, but they also have a special taste that always makes me think of her. They also make me remember my British ancestry and my mother's history. They help me connect to my past and to my family. Yorkshire pudding is such a simple and common English food, but it will always be special to me because of my mother.

1. What is the topic sentence? Underline it.

2. What is the concluding sentence? Underline it.

3. How does Yorkshire pudding taste? Circle the sentence that describes the taste.

B. Write the adjectives the writer uses to describe Yorkshire pudding. You can look at the paragraph to help you.

delicious, traditional _____

_____

_____

Adjectives are words that describe nouns (_people_, _places_, _things_, and _ideas_) and are always singular. When two or more adjectives are used before a noun, they usually follow the order given in the chart below.

Opinion/ Quality	Size	Age	Shape	Color	Origin	Material	Kind/ Purpose
beautiful	big	old	round	yellow	Chinese	glass	serving
expensive	small	new	square	green	French	leather	running

Rosario lives in a **big, old** house in the country.
We ate dinner at the **new French** restaurant in our neighborhood.
Ming gave Ella and Mike a **beautiful glass serving** dish as a wedding gift.
Eduardo bought a pair of **expensive leather running** shoes.

We do not usually use more than three adjectives before a noun. We use two or three adjectives and then add additional descriptive phrases after the noun.

Leila wore a **beautiful green silk** skirt from India.

Tip Critical Thinking

Activity A asks you to **classify** adjectives. When you classify, you put things into groups according to certain qualities or principles. **Classifying** information can help you understand it better.

A. Work with a partner. Write each adjective in the correct column of the chart on page 41.

Korean	rectangular	orange	American
oval	triangular	unusual	teenage
little	common	metal	huge
pretty	cotton	antique	medical
funny	friendly	silk	nice
lovely	ugly	wedding	elderly
glass	plastic	traditional	writing
tasty	~~cheap~~	dancing	racing
wool	Brazilian	Omani	ceramic
modern	fashionable	~~hiking~~	ancient
interesting	uncomfortable	wonderful	elegant

Opinion/Quality	Size	Age	Shape
cheap			

Color	Origin	Material	Kind/Purpose
			hiking

B. Write a sentence about each topic. Use three adjectives from different categories in each sentence. You can use adjectives from the chart in Activity A or use your own ideas.

1. your favorite dessert

_____

2. a member of your family

_____

3. something you are wearing today

_____

4. something you ate this week

_____

5. a movie or book you like

_____

6. a restaurant you like

_____

In this assignment, you are going to write a descriptive paragraph about your favorite dish. As you prepare your paragraph, think about the Unit Question, "What makes food taste good?" Refer to the Self-Assessment checklist on page 44. Use information from Readings 1 and 2 and your work in this unit to support your ideas.

For alternative unit assignments, see the *Q: Skills for Success Teacher's Handbook.*

PLAN AND WRITE

A. **BRAINSTORM**   Think about your favorite dish. Use the questions below to help brainstorm ideas about your topic.

1. What is the name of the dish?

    _____

2. How would you describe the dish? What taste(s) and ingredients does it have?

    _____

    _____

3. Does this dish have personal or cultural importance to you? Why?

    _____

    _____

4. Who usually makes this dish for you? Is it easy or difficult to make? Why?

    _____

    _____

5. How does the dish make you feel?

    _____

    _____

B. **PLAN** Use your notes from Activity A to make an outline of your ideas.

1. **Topic sentence:** Write a topic sentence that names the dish and expresses your main idea:

   Topic sentence: _____

   _____

   _____

2. **Subtopic and supporting details:** Decide which information from Activity A you will include in the body of your paragraph to support your main idea.

   A. _____

   _____

      1. _____

      2. _____

   B. _____

   _____

      1. _____

      2. _____

3. **Concluding sentence:** Write a concluding sentence that summarizes the main points of your paragraph and restates the topic sentence in different words.

   Concluding sentence: _____

   _____

   _____

C. **WRITE** Use your outline from Activity B to help you organize and write your paragraph in your notebook that describes your favorite dish. Be sure to use adjectives to make your description interesting, clear, and specific. Look at the Self-Assessment checklist on page 44 to guide your writing.

Revise and Edit

A. PEER REVIEW Read a partner's paragraph. Answer the questions and discuss them with your partner.

1. Is there a clear topic sentence? Underline it.

2. Do you have a clear idea of the ingredients in the dish and how it tastes?

3. Is it clear why this is the author's favorite dish?

4. How many adjectives does the author use to describe this dish? Underline them. Do you think there are enough adjectives?

B. REWRITE Review the answers to the questions in Activity A. You may want to revise and rewrite your paragraph.

C. EDIT Complete the Self-Assessment checklist as you prepare to write the final draft of your paragraph. Be prepared to hand in your work or discuss it in class.

Yes	No	SELF-ASSESSMENT
☐	☐	Is the punctuation correct?
☐	☐	Are all words spelled correctly?
☐	☐	Does the paragraph include vocabulary from the unit?
☐	☐	Does the paragraph include descriptive adjectives?
☐	☐	Are the adjectives in the correct order?

Circle the words and phrases you learned in this unit.

Nouns

concept 🔑 AWL
cuisine
method 🔑 AWL
portion AWL
practice 🔑
principle 🔑 AWL
property 🔑
region 🔑 AWL
system 🔑

Verbs

consume AWL
identify 🔑 AWL
influence 🔑
recognize 🔑

Adjectives

balanced
likely 🔑
sensitive 🔑

Adverb

typically 🔑

Phrases

at risk
be made up of

🔑 Oxford 3000™ words
AWL Academic Word List

Check (✓) the skills you learned. If you need more work on a skill, refer to the page(s) in parentheses.

READING ⬤	I can preview a text. (p. 32)
VOCABULARY ⬤	I can use context to understand words. (p. 37)
WRITING ⬤	I can use descriptive adjectives in writing. (p. 39)
GRAMMAR ⬤	I can use adjectives in the correct order. (p. 40)
LEARNING OUTCOME ⬤	I can write a paragraph about my favorite dish using descriptive adjectives.

UNIT 3

Success

READING ● scanning a text
VOCABULARY ● collocations
WRITING ● organizing an opinion paragraph
GRAMMAR ● subject-verb agreement

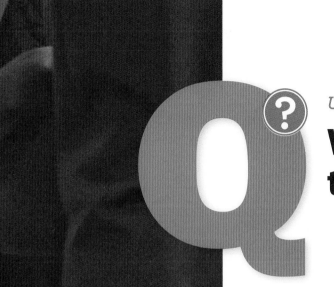

Unit QUESTION

What does it take to be successful?

PREVIEW THE UNIT

A Discuss these questions with your classmates.

How does someone become a successful athlete?

What are some things people give up or sacrifice in order to be successful?

Look at the photo. Where is the woman? Why is she lying down?

B Discuss the Unit Question above with your classmates.

Listen to *The Q Classroom*, Track 8 on CD 1, to hear other answers.

47

C Read the statements. Check (✓) whether you agree or disagree with each statement. Discuss your answers with a partner.

	Strongly Disagree	Disagree	Agree	Strongly Agree
Great athletes should make more than a million dollars a year.	◯	◯	◯	◯
Being an athlete involves sacrifice or personal costs.	◯	◯	◯	◯
It's OK for sports teams to ask companies for money to help them train.	◯	◯	◯	◯
Parents should push their children to play sports.	◯	◯	◯	◯
Children should not play sports that can hurt them.	◯	◯	◯	◯

Tip Critical Thinking

Activity D includes an idea map, which is a kind of diagram. When you **diagram** your ideas, you are analyzing how those ideas are connected to each other. Understanding those connections can help you speak and write more clearly.

D Write the name of your favorite sport in the idea map. Think about the costs or the sacrifices someone needs to make in order to be successful at it. Write your ideas in the idea map. Then discuss your answers with your partner.

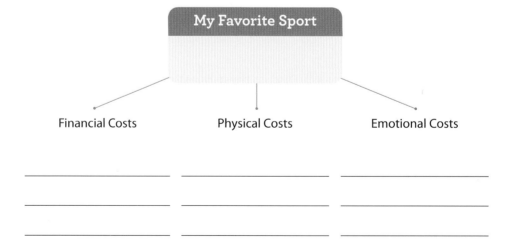

My Favorite Sport

Financial Costs   Physical Costs   Emotional Costs

_____   _____   _____

_____   _____   _____

_____   _____   _____

READING 1 | Fast Cars, Big Money

VOCABULARY

Here are some words from Reading 1. Read the sentences. Circle the word or phrase that can replace the bold word without changing the meaning of the sentence.

1. A company **logo** usually gives the full name of the company or the first letter of the name. (symbol / address / rule)

2. Many companies choose to **sponsor** sports teams so that they can advertise on their uniforms. (support / watch / buy)

3. A brand-new business cannot be **assured** that it will succeed right away. (worried / sure / interested)

4. Businesses need to make **profits** in order to be successful. (income / friends / decisions)

5. When companies **invest** money to make a new product, they have to consider the costs carefully. (need / lose / spend)

6. The Internet has given businesses access to a bigger **market** around the world. (number of customers / number of difficulties / number of computers)

7. Large companies generally have more **stability** than small businesses. (choice / strength / problems)

8. It is wise to invest in **dependable** companies because they tend to manage their money well. (new / reliable / different)

9. There has been a large **expansion** in the number of bilingual jobs because of the global economy. (decrease / growth / cost)

10. In order to be successful, a business needs to consider its **image**, or the way the public sees it. (attitude / appearance / growth)

PREVIEW READING 1

You are going to read an article from a business magazine about the popular sport of car racing from a business perspective.

Read the headings. What do you think is the purpose of the article? Check (✓) your answer.

☐ to explain the sport of Formula 1 car racing
☐ to encourage businesses to invest in car racing

CD 1
Track 9   **Read the article.**

Fast Cars, Big Money

Does your business need a boost?

1   Imagine 350 million people seeing your company **logo** every year. Imagine that number growing even higher every year. Imagine being part of one of the most prestigious[1] and glamorous[2] sports in the world and making millions of dollars at the same time. Sound attractive? Hundreds of companies have already discovered the financial benefits of **sponsoring** Formula 1 racing. When you choose to sponsor a team, you can be **assured** that your company will grow financially and globally.

Why are companies interested?

2   Companies have realized that investments in the sport of auto racing can bring them huge **profits**. Businesses, including banks, hotels, and telecommunication companies, **invest** tens of millions of dollars every year to sponsor race teams. Hundreds of millions of people watch car races every year. For companies, this is an enormous **market**.

3   Cars race around the track with company logos stuck to the doors, hood, and trunk, and people notice. Corporate sponsors can invest $5 million in a race team and make $30 million or more from car advertising. The costs are cheap compared to the profits. Sponsoring a team also shows the financial **stability** of your company. Race cars can cost tens of millions of dollars, and race teams can spend up to $300 million a year. Companies who invest in race teams are showing the world that they are powerful and **dependable**.

Why is investing now a good idea?

4   Much of Formula 1's current success comes from its **expansion** to global markets. Although most races are in Europe, today there are races in the Middle East and Asia. Companies support worldwide expansion because it gives them new

Formula 1 race car

---

[1] **prestigious:** respected or admired because of success
[2] **glamorous:** attractive or full of glamor

customers in emerging markets. They can push their brand[3] globally. Many companies have already invested in Formula 1's most recent host locations, including Bahrain, Abu Dhabi, and Singapore. As a result, they have been able to expand their business to the Middle East and Asia. These areas of the world are full of business opportunities, and Formula 1 racing has brought them more growth and success. Expanding overseas also shows that your company has a global message, which is important in today's global economy.

Why should my company invest?

5   Thanks to a strong business mentality, Formula 1 racing has become a profitable sport for corporations to invest in. The global economy is always changing, but the industry has succeeded by finding new ways to make more money. Sponsoring a team will not only bring your company profits, but will also improve your company's **image** as a business that is stable and global-minded. Take advantage of this wonderful business opportunity, and enjoy being part of this glamorous, thrill-seeking[4] sport. Vroom vroom!

[3] **brand:** the name of a product that is made by a particular company

[4] **thrill-seeking:** trying to find pleasure in excitement

MAIN IDEAS

Read the sentences. Write the correct paragraph number next to each main idea.

_1_ **a.** By sponsoring a Formula 1 team, a company will grow financially and globally.

____ **b.** Formula 1 sponsorship is profitable and shows that a company is powerful and reliable.

____ **c.** Sponsors can make a lot of money from car advertising.

____ **d.** Formula 1 racing is a good investment today because of its expansion to global markets.

____ **e.** Sponsorship brings companies profits and improves their image.

DETAILS

Cross out the incorrect answer.

1. Why should companies be interested in advertising with Formula 1?
    a. Investing in Formula 1 racing makes a company look powerful.
    b. The costs of investing are higher than the profits.
    c. Millions of people will see a company's advertisements.
    d. Corporate sponsorship shows a business is dependable.

2. What are some other reasons that companies should invest in Formula 1 racing?

   a. Formula 1 racing is a fun and glamorous sport for everyone.

   b. Companies can make a lot of money from Formula 1 racing.

   c. Sponsorship will improve a company's global image.

   d. Sponsoring a race team shows that a company is dependable.

3. Why is investing now a good idea?

   a. Formula 1 racing is expanding to the Middle East and Asia.

   b. Companies can advertise in emerging markets.

   c. A global message is important in today's economy.

   d. Companies can push their brand in Europe.

 ## WHAT DO YOU THINK?

Discuss the questions in a group. Then choose one question and write five to eight sentences in response.

1. Do you think sponsoring Formula 1 racing is a good or bad investment? Explain.

2. Do you think that businesses that sponsor sports like car racing would be as successful without giving sponsorship money? Why or why not?

| Reading Skill | Scanning a text | |

Scanning means looking through a text quickly to find specific information, such as names, numbers, and dates. We scan items like the newspaper, a timetable, a dictionary, and the table of contents in a book. When you scan, do not read every word. Look for key words or phrases that will help you find the answer quickly. Think about how the information will appear on the page. For example, if you are looking for a date, scan only for numbers.

A. Scan Reading 1 for the missing information. Use keys words in the sentences to help you find the answers. Then complete each statement.

1. Businesses that sponsor race teams include _____,

   _____, and _____.

2. Company logos are stuck to the _____, _____,

   and _____ of race cars.

3. Although most Formula 1 races are in Europe, today there are races in

_____ and _____.

4. Formula 1's most recent host locations include _____,

_____ and _____.

B. Scan Reading 1 again for the missing numbers. Use key words in the sentences to help you find the answers. Then complete each statement.

1. Every year, _____ million people watch Formula 1 races.

2. Businesses invest _____ of _____ of dollars every year to sponsor race teams.

3. Corporate sponsors can invest just _____ in a race team and make more than _____ from their logos on cars.

4. Race teams can spend up to _____ a year.

READING 2 | Practice Makes ... Pain?

VOCABULARY

Here are some words and phrases from Reading 2. Read the sentences. Circle the answer that best matches the meaning of each bold word or phrase.

1. Ice skating is a **demanding** sport that requires a lot of time, practice, and hard work.
   a. difficult   b. expensive   c. harmful

2. Putting kids in sports at a young age is a growing **trend** in many countries today.
   a. new profession   b. general change   c. high cost

3. We cancelled the soccer game **due to** the rain. It was too wet and dangerous to play.
   a. because of   b. in order to   c. late for

4. The official made a **motion** with his hand to let the runners know it was time to start the race.
   a. ticket   b. movement   c. question

5. Athletes who play sports **aggressively** get hurt more frequently than athletes who don't.
   a. forcefully   b. quietly   c. quickly

6. Most competitive athletes earn money for playing sports, but gymnasts are an **exception**. They do not receive a salary.
   a. new rule   b. someone not included   c. professional athlete

7. Competitive athletes must have **dedication** because it takes a lot of time and hard work to be successful in sports.
   a. money   b. skill   c. commitment

8. Sore muscles are a **sign** that you have exercised very hard.
   a. signal   b. injury   c. sacrifice

9. It can take months for an athlete to **recover** from a serious injury.
   a. compete   b. get better   c. get sick

PREVIEW READING 2

This is an online article. It is about child athletes and what they do to succeed in sports. Look at the title. What do you think the writer will say about child athletes?

Check (✓) your answer.

☐ It's easy for children to be successful in sports if they start early.

☐ The sacrifices children make for success in sports are sometimes too great.

 CD 1 Track 10   **Read the article.**

Practice Makes ... Pain?

1   At 10, Courtney Thompson was a top-ranked gymnast in New Hampshire. She had been doing flips since she was one and had her heart set on competing in the Olympics. She practiced four and a half hours a day, six days a week, often repeating the same move 100 times. Her **demanding** schedule took a toll[1]. It got to the point where Courtney could barely straighten her elbows unless she put ice on them. On January 12, 2005, she had to

[1] **take a toll:** to have a negative effect

Young gymnast

stop in the middle of a floor routine. "I jumped up and grabbed my arm. It hurt really bad."

2   Doctors discovered that Courtney's constant workouts had caused the cartilage, or connective tissue, in her elbow to separate from the bone. She had surgery on both arms and went though months of painful rehabilitation². Courtney's experience is part of a growing **trend** in youth sports—kids and teens were starting to have the same type of injuries that only professional athletes used to have. Experts say kids are pushing their bodies to the limit, practicing sports too hard for too long. The exhausting schedules often lead to dangerous injuries that could keep young athletes from competing—permanently.

Under Strain

3   According to experts at *The Physician and Sportsmedicine* journal, between 30 and 50 percent of youth sports injuries are **due to** overuse. Overuse injuries are caused by repetitive **motion** that, over time, puts more stress on a body part than it can handle. The tissue or bone eventually breaks, stretches, or tears.

4   Danny Clark ended up with an overuse injury last year. The teen baseball player from Altamonte Springs, Florida, hurt himself by throwing 80 pitches in a single game after two months of not pitching at all. The sudden repetitive action tore Danny's rotator cuff. The rotator cuff is a group of four muscles and the tendons that connect them to bones in the shoulder. Afterward, he couldn't pitch for two months and needed five months of physical therapy.

Too Much, Too Soon

5   Experts say injuries such as Danny's are on the rise, in part because more and more kids are leaving casual sports for organized team competitions that require hours of practice and game time. "Kids [are] playing sports more **aggressively** at younger ages," explains James Beaty, an orthopedist in Memphis, Tennessee.

6   Kevin Butcher, a 15-year-old soccer player from Fort Collins, Colorado, is no **exception**. He plays soccer three or four times a week for nine months a year. His **dedication** pays off—last year he helped lead his team to a state championship. But his success came with a price. "Last year, I sprained my ankle a few times, dislocated³ a bone in my foot, and broke both sides of my pelvis⁴," Kevin says. The first time he broke his pelvis, Kevin didn't realize it for about a month. He played through the pain until doctors forced him to rest. When he dislocated a bone in his foot, a physical therapist put the bone into place, bandaged his foot, and let him play the next day.

---

² **rehabilitation:** the process of returning to a normal life again after an injury

³ **dislocate:** to put a bone out of its correct position

⁴ **pelvis:** the set of wide bones at the bottom of your back that connect to your legs

Children playing soccer

Knowing Your Limits

7   Not every kid who plays sports ends up with serious injuries. Experts say the key to avoiding injury is paying attention to your body. Feeling sore after practice is OK, but sharp pain is a warning **sign** that shouldn't be ignored. Kevin learned that lesson while **recovering** from his second broken pelvis in less than a year. "There's definitely a glory in playing through pain, but I think there is a limit. You just have to know when to stop."

MAIN IDEAS

Look back at the reading. Then complete the statements.

1. Children in youth sports have more injuries today because

_____.

2. Many injuries are due to _____.

3. Organized team competitions cause more injuries because

_____.

4. Child athletes can avoid injury by _____.

DETAILS

Scan Reading 2. Complete the chart with the missing information.

	Name	Home	Sport	Injury
1.	Courtney Thompson	New Hampshire		
2.			baseball player	
3.				sprained ankle, dislocated bone, broken pelvis

WHAT DO YOU THINK?

A. Discuss the questions in a group. Then choose one question and write five to eight sentences in response.

1. Do you think competing in sports is good for young children? Explain.

2. Do you think coaches and parents have a responsibility to try to stop children from getting hurt while doing sports? Why or why not?

B. Think about both Reading 1 and Reading 2 as you discuss the questions.

1. What are some ways that athletes pay for success?

2. How do parents of child athletes pay for success? Consider financial, physical, and psychological costs in your response.

Vocabulary Skill | Collocations web⁺

Tip for Success

A collocations dictionary lists collocations alphabetically for easy reference. Use a collocations dictionary to help you identify and learn new collocations.

Collocations are words that frequently go together. One common pattern for collocations is adjective + preposition.

Adjective	+	Preposition	Adjective	+	Preposition
interested		in	famous		for
due		to	upset		about

Learning collocations will help you increase your vocabulary and improve your writing.

A. Complete each sentence with the correct adjective + preposition collocation.

afraid of	interested in	sure about
due to	involved in	upset about
famous for	nervous about	

1. Parents whose children compete in sports are often _____*afraid*_____ ___*of*___ injuries.

2. The player's injury was _____ _____ overuse.

3. Carlos was not _____ _____ the meaning of the word, so he looked it up in the dictionary.

4. Felix was very _____ _____ losing the championship game. He really wanted to win.

5. Nadia Comăneci is _____ _____ being one of the greatest gymnasts in history.

6. More children are _____ _____ professional sports at a very young age today. My neighbor's daughter started playing soccer when she was four.

7. Are you _____ _____ going to the baseball game tonight? I have an extra ticket if you'd like to go.

8. The gymnast was _____ _____ competing for the first time in front of hundreds of people.

B. Write five sentences using adjective + preposition collocations from Activity A.

1. _____

   _____

2. _____

   _____

3. _____

   _____

4. _____

   _____

5. _____

   _____

WRITING

An **opinion paragraph** is a paragraph in which you explain how you feel about a topic. For example, you might explain whether you agree or disagree with a particular idea. The goal of writing an opinion paragraph is to help the reader understand your opinion. Begin your opinion paragraph with a topic sentence that clearly expresses your opinion. Then give reasons and examples that support your opinion. End your paragraph with a concluding sentence that restates your opinion.

Topic sentence: Competing on a sports team helps children learn important life skills.

Reason 1: They learn to be responsible.

Example: When children play on a team, they have to be on time and work hard.

Reason 2: They learn to work on a team.

Example: On a team, children learn how to make decisions as a group.

Concluding sentence: Children learn many valuable skills by playing sports.

A. Read the opinion paragraph. What is the writer's opinion of Kung fu? Underline the topic sentence. Then put a check mark (✓) next to the reasons and examples.

Kung Fu

Kung fu is the perfect sport for young children. First of all, it does not cost much to participate. For example, a typical uniform is less than fifty dollars, and weekly lessons are not expensive compared to other sports. In addition, children learn the benefits of discipline and setting goals. The colored belts for completing a level keep kids motivated, and each child is able to succeed at his or her own pace. Finally, Kung fu teaches children how to protect themselves in the real world. Children do not learn to fight but acquire important moves and motions that they can use to defend themselves if necessary. Kung fu not only is cheap, but also teaches many important skills and lessons. For these reasons, parents should consider Kung fu as a sport for their children.

Kung fu teaches many important skills.

B. Complete the outline with information from the paragraph in Activity A. Discuss your answers with a partner.

1. **Topic sentence:** _____

2. **Reasons and examples:**

   Reason 1: _First of all, it does not cost much to participate._____

      Example: _____

   Reason 2: _____

      Example: _____

   Reason 3: _____

      Example: _____

3. **Concluding sentence:** _____

   _____

Grammar   Subject-verb agreement   web

Subject-verb agreement is important when using the simple present.

Singular subjects with the simple present

When the subject of a sentence is singular, the verb should be singular. For negative statements, use *does not* + the base form of the verb.

> She **plays** soccer three times a week.
> He **pitches** 80 times a game.
> It **does not cost** much to participate.

Plural subjects with the simple present

When the subject is plural, the verb should plural. For negative statements, use *do not* + the base form.

> The colored <u>belts</u> **motivate** kids.
> <u>They</u> **practice** five days a week.
> <u>They</u> **do not learn** to fight.

To check for subject-verb agreement, it is helpful to replace a noun with the pronoun *it* or *they*.

Kung fu = "it"

The instructors = "they"

The simple present of *be*

Remember that the simple present of *be* has different forms for singular and plural subjects.

> Kung fu **is** the perfect sport for children.
> The instructors **are** very experienced.
> Ice dancing **isn't** an easy sport.
> Weekly lessons **are not** expensive.

Remember, some nouns have a singular form, but refer to a group of people. These are called **collective nouns**. Collective nouns usually take singular verbs.

> The government **makes** laws.
> The soccer team **practices** every day after school.

A. Read the paragraph. Correct the ten mistakes in subject-verb agreement. The first one has been done for you.

Beauty and Sacrifice

Ice dancing is a beautiful sport, but it ~~require~~ requires a number of sacrifices. For young dancers, most days is composed of skating, school, and homework. Competitive dancers needs to practice for five to six hours every day. Dancers usually skate early in the morning, so they always need to go to bed early. A dancer who do not get enough sleep will not perform well. In addition, ice dancing cost a lot of money. Dancers must pay for lessons, ice time, and costumes, which can be thousands of dollars. This make the sport very expensive. Ice dancing are also difficult on the body. If dancers does not skate carefully, they can get hurt. Many dancers gets injuries from falling on the ice or repeating the same motions too many times. It is not easy being a competitive ice dancer, but the sacrifices is worth it to those who love this glamorous sport.

B. Complete each sentence with simple present of the verb in parentheses. Then compare your answers with a partner.

1. Many parents _____think_____ (think) that gymnastics is a good sport for young girls.

2. The race car _____ (have) a company logo on its door.

3. Dedication _____ (be) very important in sports.

4. Children _____ (need) their parents' support when they compete in sports.

5. Baseball players _____ (make) a lot of money when they become famous.

6. Overuse injuries _____ (be) more common in child athletes today.

7. It _____ (cost) millions of dollars to sponsor a Formula 1 racing team.

8. Our team _____ (practice) for two hours every Saturday.

Unit Assignment   **Write an opinion paragraph**

In this assignment, you are going to write an opinion paragraph on one of the topics below. As you prepare your paragraph, think about the Unit Question, "What does it take to be successful?" Refer to the Self-Assessment checklist on page 64. Use information from Readings 1 and 2 and your work in this unit to support your ideas.

For alternative unit assignments, see the *Q: Skills for Success Teacher's Handbook*.

1. Should athletes or sports teams accept money from corporate sponsors in order to be successful? Discuss one or more specific sports in your paragraph.

2. Should child athletes be pushed hard in order to succeed? Discuss one or more specific sports in your paragraph.

PLAN AND WRITE

A. **BRAINSTORM** Choose one of the topics from page 62 and think about your answer or opinion about the topic. Then follow the steps below.

1. Write your opinion about the topic.

   _____

   _____

2. Brainstorm as many ideas as you can about the topic you chose in your notebook.

 **Your Writing Process**

For this activity, you could also use Stage 1B, *Talking About Your Ideas* in *Q Online Practice*.

B. **PLAN** Follow these steps to plan your paragraph.

1. Read your notes from Activity A. Circle any ideas or examples that support your opinion.

2. Write an outline for your paragraph.

   A. **Topic sentence:** Write a topic sentence that clearly expresses your opinion.

   _____

   _____

   _____

   B. **Reasons and examples:** List reasons and examples to support your opinion.

   Reason 1: _____

   _____

       Example: _____

   Reason 2: _____

   _____

       Example: _____

   Reason 3: _____

   _____

       Example: _____

C. **Concluding sentence:** Write a concluding sentence that restates your opinion.

_____

_____

_____

C. WRITE Write your paragraph in your notebook. Use your outline from Activity B. Use collocations with adjectives and prepositions. Look at the Self-Assessment checklist below to guide your writing.

REVISE AND EDIT

A. PEER REVIEW Read a partner's paragraph. Answer the questions and discuss them with your partner.

1. Is the opinion clearly expressed in the paragraph?

2. Is there a clear topic sentence? Underline it.

3. Are there reasons and examples to support the writer's opinion?

4. Is there a concluding sentence? Underline it.

B. REWRITE Review the answers to the questions in Activity A. You may want to revise and rewrite your paragraph.

C. EDIT Complete the Self-Assessment checklist as you prepare to write the final draft of your paragraph. Be prepared to hand in your work or discuss it in class.

SELF-ASSESSMENT		
Yes	No	
☐	☐	Is the punctuation correct?
☐	☐	Are all words spelled correctly?
☐	☐	Does the paragraph include vocabulary from the unit?
☐	☐	Are adjective + preposition collocations used correctly?
☐	☐	Is the subject-verb agreement correct?

Circle the words and phrases you learned in this unit.

Nouns	Verbs	Collocations
dedication	invest 🔑 AWL	afraid of
exception 🔑	recover 🔑 AWL	due to 🔑
expansion AWL	sponsor	famous for
image 🔑 AWL		interested in
logo	**Adjectives**	involved in 🔑
market 🔑	assured AWL	nervous about
motion 🔑	demanding	sure about
profit 🔑	dependable	upset about
sign 🔑		
stability AWL	**Adverb**	
trend 🔑 AWL	aggressively	

🔑 Oxford 3000™ words

AWL Academic Word List

Check (✓) the skills you learned. If you need more work on a skill, refer to the page(s) in parentheses.

READING ●	I can scan a text. (p. 52)
VOCABULARY ●	I can use collocations with adjectives + prepositions. (p. 57)
WRITING ●	I can organize an opinion paragraph. (p. 59)
GRAMMAR ●	I can use subject-verb agreement. (pp. 60–61)
LEARNING OUTCOME ●	I can state and support my personal perspectives in an "opinion" paragraph.

READING	●	taking notes
VOCABULARY	●	synonyms
WRITING	●	writing a summary
GRAMMAR	●	parallel structure

New Perspectives

LEARNING OUTCOME •

Write a paragraph summarizing a reading text and an opinion paragraph in response to the text.

Unit QUESTION

How has technology affected your life?

PREVIEW THE UNIT

(A) **Discuss these questions with your classmates.**

What do you like to do in your free time?

How do you use technology in your daily life?

Look at the photo. What are the different kinds of technology the man is using? What is he doing?

(B) **Discuss the Unit Question above with your classmates.**

⟩⟩ **Listen to *The Q Classroom*, Track 11 on CD 1, to hear other answers.**

C Complete the questionnaire. Then discuss your answers with a partner.

How do you spend your free time?

How many hours a week do you spend doing each of these activities?

1. chatting online
- ☐ 0–5 hours
- ☐ 5–10 hours
- ☐ 10–15 hours
- ☐ 15–20 hours
- ☐ 20+ hours

3. playing sports/exercising
- ☐ 0–5 hours
- ☐ 5–10 hours
- ☐ 10–15 hours
- ☐ 15–20 hours
- ☐ 20+ hours

5. surfing the Internet
- ☐ 0–5 hours
- ☐ 5–10 hours
- ☐ 10–15 hours
- ☐ 15–20 hours
- ☐ 20+ hours

2. spending time with friends
- ☐ 0–5 hours
- ☐ 5–10 hours
- ☐ 10–15 hours
- ☐ 15–20 hours
- ☐ 20+ hours

4. reading
- ☐ 0–5 hours
- ☐ 5–10 hours
- ☐ 10–15 hours
- ☐ 15–20 hours
- ☐ 20+ hours

6. watching TV
- ☐ 0–5 hours
- ☐ 5–10 hours
- ☐ 10–15 hours
- ☐ 15–20 hours
- ☐ 20+ hours

D The chart below shows how people around the world spend their free time. It shows the average number of hours per week people from different countries spend doing each activity. Look at the chart. Then discuss the questions with a partner.

	TV	Radio	Internet	Reading
Mexico	11.6	11.1	6.3	5.5
Saudi Arabia	17.7	3.9	9.3	6.8
Spain	15.9	9.9	11.5	5.8
Thailand	22.4	13.3	11.7	9.4
United States	19	10.2	8.8	5.7
Global average	16.6	8	8.9	6.5

Source: Tracy Baker, *First Glimpse* magazine, 2005

1. Compare the global averages in the chart to the amount of time you spend doing the same activities. Are they similar or different?

2. Does any information in the chart surprise you? Explain.

READING

READING 1 | Having a Second Life

VOCABULARY

Here are some words from Reading 1. Read their definitions. Then complete each sentence.

> **benefit** (*n.*) an advantage or useful effect that something has
>
> **explore** (*v.*) to travel around a place in order to learn about it
>
> **fantasy** (*n.*) a situation that is not true, that you just imagine
>
> **interact** (*v.*) to communicate or mix with someone, especially while you work, play, or spend time together
>
> **limitation** (*n.*) a condition that controls or restricts what you can do
>
> **realistic** (*adj.*) not real but appearing to be real
>
> **social** (*adj.*) connected with meeting people and enjoying yourself
>
> **transaction** (*n.*) an exchange or transfer of goods, services, or funds
>
> **virtual** (*adj.*) made to appear to exist by the use of computer software; for example, on the Internet

1. Some video games take place in imaginary worlds that look nothing like the real world. In contrast, others are more _____.

2. In the past, students had to visit colleges to see what they looked like, but today many colleges let you _____ their campuses online.

3. You don't have to leave home to see new places. You can just go online and take a(n) _____ tour of almost any city.

4. Always make sure a website is safe and secure before making a(n) _____ such as paying a bill or buying something.

5. My parents worry that I spend too much time on the Internet. They want me to _____ with my friends in the real world, not online.

6. Nowadays, people can have two different _____ lives—one with friends they visit and another with friends they talk to online.

7. Many online games present a world of _____, which often includes made-up situations and strange creatures.

8. One _____ of shopping online is that I can do it at home, but the disadvantage is that I don't go out as much anymore!

9. If you don't pay for a membership to the website, you can't read all the articles. There's a(n) _____ on how much information you can access without paying.

PREVIEW READING 1

You are going to read an article from a computer magazine that describes a social website called Second Life. Second Life offers users, or "residents," a huge online community and virtual world.

Read the first sentence of each paragraph. Why do you think people use this site? Write your ideas.

_____

_____

_____

Having a Second Life

1   As computer technology has improved, today's online environments have become more complex and **realistic**. One website that has attracted over six million Internet users is Second Life. Second Life is a three-dimensional (3-D)[1] online world where people work, shop, sell and trade items, meet others, go to concerts, and much more. Users, who are called "residents," create their own characters, or "avatars." They use their avatars to **explore** Second Life's **virtual** world.

2   Just like any country, Second Life has its own economy. Using a credit card, users can buy "Linden Dollars," the official currency of Second Life. With Linden Dollars, they can buy land or even an entire island where they can build and decorate their own house, start a garden, or even set up their own store. Land is treated as a valuable commodity[2] in Second Life. Residents can choose to rent or sell their land to other users, and they can earn real money from these **transactions**. Some users

Users can buy an entire island on Second Life.

have reported making tens of thousands of dollars from selling Second Life real estate[3].

3   When residents want to be **social** (and most of them do), they can use their avatars to **interact** with others. There are games, shopping malls, clubs, and many kinds of stores available to residents. Avatars can also attend conferences, art shows, and concerts. Real rock bands, such as the British pop group Duran Duran, have even given live concerts on Second Life. With so many opportunities for interesting things to do and see, it's easy to see why so many users spend so much time on the site.

4   Second Life offers users a quick and easy escape from the real world. Many residents see this as one of the main **benefits** of using the site. Spending time on Second Life allows them to escape the stresses and problems of their daily lives. If a user is having a stressful day at work, she can visit a beautiful island, go skiing, or even fly to another planet during her lunch break. If she is tired at the end of a long day, she can go to a classical music concert while dinner is cooking and never leave home. Users can even visit other planets to help them forget their "first-life" problems for a little while.

5   In addition to escaping the stress of their daily lives, users can also escape who they are in the real world and live out their **fantasies**. For example, residents can change their occupations, physical appearance, and even their nationalities. A doctor from the United States can be a Brazilian musician on Second Life, or a banker can choose to be an Olympic

---

[1] **three-dimensional (3-D):** having or appearing to have length, width, and height
[2] **commodity:** something that you buy or sell

[3] **real estate:** property that cannot be moved, such as land and buildings

basketball player. Basically, Second Life lets users live in a world without **limitations**. This is very exciting to many people.

6   Although Second Life started as a way for people to escape the real world, it has become more and more like the real world in many ways. Now on Second Life, some countries have virtual embassies, businesses have meetings in virtual rooms, and universities have places where students can view the campus and take classes. Today, Second Life allows users to experience both fantasy and reality in the same place.

MAIN IDEAS

Read the sentences. Then number them in the order that the ideas appear in Reading 1.

____ a.   Second Life allows people to escape their real lives.

____ b.   Second Life has become more like the real world.

____ c.   Second Life has its own money system.

____ d.   Second Life lets a person be someone else for a while.

____ e.   Second Life provides entertainment and ways to meet others.

DETAILS

Answer these questions. Look back at Reading 1 to help you. Then discuss your answers with a partner.

1.   How can people make real money on Second Life?

_____

2.   What kinds of realistic places can residents visit?

_____

3.   What are some things users can do to escape their daily lives?

_____

4.   How has Second Life become more like the real world?

_____

5.   How are universities using Second Life today?

_____

Q WHAT DO YOU THINK?

Discuss the questions in a group. Then choose one question and write five to eight sentences in response.

1. What positive and negative effects do you think a website like Second Life can have on people?

2. Would you consider joining a website like Second Life? Why or why not?

| Reading Skill | Taking notes | |

Taking notes while you are reading will help you become a more active reader. To take notes, write on the text and next to the text. Your notes should help you identify important ideas. You should:

- Underline or highlight topics and main ideas
- Underline supporting **details** and the most important words and phrases
- Focus on content words like nouns, verbs, and adjectives
- Summarize the main idea of each paragraph in the margin—don't use complete sentences

Reviewing your notes can help you remember important concepts. Use your notes to prepare for a class or an exam.

A. Read the first paragraph of Reading 1 below. Look at the student's notes. Then discuss the questions with a partner.

*Second Life →
online "other" world*

As computer technology has improved, <u>today's online environments</u> have become <u>more complex and realistic</u>. One website that has attracted over six million Internet users is Second Life. <u>Second Life</u> is a <u>three-dimensional (3-D) online world</u> where people work, shop, sell and trade items, meet others, go to concerts, and much more. <u>Users</u>, who are called "<u>residents</u>," create their own <u>characters</u>, or "<u>avatars</u>." They use their avatars to explore Second Life's virtual world.

1. What types of words did the student underline?

_____

_____

2. Look at the words and ideas the student did not underline. Why are they less important?

_____

_____

3. Look at the note in the margin. What does the note summarize?

_____

_____

_____

4. What is the main idea of the paragraph? How do you know?

_____

_____

_____

B. Reread Reading 1. Take notes using ideas from the Reading Skill box. Then compare your notes with a partner.

READING 2 | Living Outside the Box

VOCABULARY

Here are some words from Reading 2. Read their definitions. Then complete the email message. Use each word once.

confession (*n.*) a statement that you have done something bad, wrong, or unexpected

discover (*v.*) to find or learn something new or unexpected

eventually (*adv.*) in the end; after a long time

experiment (*n.*) a scientific test that is done in order to prove something or get new knowledge

lifestyle (*n.*) the way that you live

occasion (*n.*) a particular time when something happens

rare (*adj.*) not done, seen, or happening very often

regret (*v.*) to feel sorry that you did something or that you did not do something

survive (*v.*) to continue to exist, especially in or after a difficult situation

From:	Megan Morris
To:	Laura Jones
Subject:	Goodbye cell phone!

Hey Laura,

You haven't heard from me for a while. I'm emailing you because I have lost my cell phone. But don't worry! In fact, I have to make a(n) _____ (1) : I don't miss it at all! Losing it allowed me to _____ (2) that I am happier without it! At first, I didn't think I could _____ (3) without having my cell phone always with me. I used to have it with me all the time—even at the beach and at the movies. I used it to take photos at every special _____ (4) , like my cousin's wedding. I did consider buying a new one at first, but then I thought it would be fun to be one of those _____ (5) people who doesn't own a cell phone. It was my own little _____ (6) . I wanted to test myself. _____ (7) , I found that I was happier—and safer— without it. I don't drive and text anymore, and I have more time for myself. I don't _____ (8) my decision to live cell-free. In fact, I love my new _____ (9) . Talk to you soon—just don't call my cell!

Miss you lots,

Megan

PREVIEW READING 2

You are going to read an article from an online newspaper. In the article, the author describes her experiences living without a television for one full winter.

Read the title and look at the photographs. Do you think the author will say that giving up watching TV was a positive or negative experience? Check (✓) your answer.

☐ positive
☐ negative

Living Outside the Box

1   I once unplugged the TV for a month. It was summer, the season of long walks, barbecues, and reruns. But I knew if I really wanted to prove I could avoid evening television, I'd have to **survive** a New England winter without it. In the darkest, coldest months, I would no longer be able to escape. This winter, I had my test.

2   A year ago I moved into my own place. It was just a few minutes away from my former roommate—and her television. Friends offered me a spare TV, but I said no. Living alone was an opportunity to choose how I wanted to live. And I thought that being TV-free would help me do all those things I wanted to do but didn't have time for.

3   I wondered if I would feel lonely, but decided it would be better not to try to spend time with my "friends" on TV. In the first month or so, I got away from my favorite shows by visiting real friends. **Eventually**, I didn't know what TV shows were on when. I could no longer join in conversations at my office about popular shows.

4   I kept telling people it was an **experiment**: "We'll see how it goes this winter," I'd say. I considered buying a small TV to keep in the closet and bring out on special **occasions**. But for all I was missing, I could feel positive changes. I found myself reading lots of books. I had thought that I was too tired to read after a long day at work, but not too tired to watch TV. Now I had more time to read and sleep. I also started doing volunteer work almost every week instead of every few months. I called friends who usually heard from me only at the holidays. Sometimes I even enjoyed that **rare** thing called quiet.

5   The goal wasn't to give up all entertainment. I can play DVDs on my laptop, so when a blizzard was on its way, I lined up in a video store with everybody else. Instead of channel-surfing and watching something I would later **regret**, I caught

up on some great films. I found myself resensitized[1]. I was no longer watching images without noticing their speed.

6   Sometime during the winter, the season I thought would be the most difficult, I **discovered** I had crossed the line from experiment to **lifestyle**. Finally, I put up a painting on the only living room wall that could have a TV. A friend came over for the first time, took the tour, and then sat down on the couch with a slightly puzzled look. Looking around the room, she asked, "So, don't you have a TV?"

7   Whenever I explain my TV-free home, I tell people I'm not judging anyone else's TV-viewing choices (after all, I'm glad my friends don't mind me sitting in front of their screens every once in a while). The response is often a **confession**. For example, one co-worker said she can't help turning her TV on for background noise when her husband is out of town. Others express camaraderie[2], saying they hardly ever turn theirs on.

8   I don't know how long my new lifestyle will last. I might suddenly want to reconnect with pop culture and documentaries. And if I have children, I think I'd want them to learn, as I did from my parents, how to view with moderation[3] and a critical[4] eye. But if I do make space for a TV someday, I'm more confident now that I'll still find time and space for me.

[1] **resensitized:** feeling more sensitive or emotional again
[2] **camaraderie:** a feeling of friendship and closeness

[3] **moderation:** the quality of being able to control your feelings or actions
[4] **critical:** describing the good and bad points of a play, movie, TV show, book, work of art, and so on

MAIN IDEAS

Read the sentences. Then number them in the order that the ideas appear in Reading 2.

____ a.   She started to notice positive changes in her life.

____ b.   She lived without TV for a month.

____ c.   She's confident that she can watch TV in moderation now.

____ d.   She decided to live alone, so she could choose how to live.

DETAILS

Read the statements. Write *T* (true) or *F* (false). Then correct each false statement to make it true.

_F_ 1.   She first stopped watching TV in the ~~winter~~. *(summer)*

____ 2.   Her family offered her an extra TV.

____ 3.   She did not know when her favorite shows were on.

____ 4.   She considered putting a small TV in her closet.

____ 5.   She started doing volunteer work every few months.

____ 6.   She is sure that she will buy a television in the future.

 WHAT DO YOU THINK?

A. **Discuss the questions in a group.**

1.   Would you consider escaping from television for a month or more? Why or why not?

2.   Besides television, what kind of technology would be most difficult for you to live without? Why?

B. **Think about both Reading 1 and Reading 2 as you discuss the questions. Then choose one question and write five to eight sentences in response.**

1.   What positive and negative effects can technology have on people's lives?

2.   Is visiting friends more enjoyable than chatting online with friends? Why or why not?

Synonyms are words that have similar meanings. Learning synonyms will increase your vocabulary and will give your writing more variety.

> People's <u>lifestyles</u> have changed because of the Internet.
> People's <u>habits and behaviors</u> have changed because of the Internet.

Be careful when choosing synonyms because they do not always have exactly the same meaning. A synonym can have a more general meaning or a more specific meaning.

> **General:** Millions of <u>transactions</u> occur on the Internet every day.
> **Specific:** Millions of people make <u>purchases</u> on the Internet every day.

Transactions is more general because it can mean buying or selling. *Purchases* is more specific because it means buying only.

Tip for Success

A **thesaurus** is a book that lists synonyms. Remember that words can have multiple meanings. When you check a thesaurus, make sure you look for the correct synonym for the word.

A. Rewrite each sentence by replacing the bold word or phrase with the correct synonym from the box.

benefits	experiments	rare
~~discovered~~	limitations	realistic
eventually		

1. Millions of people have **found** the online world of Second Life.

   Millions of people have discovered the online world of Second Life.

2. Second Life's gaming experience is **lifelike** due to its high-tech graphics.

   _____

3. Are there any **disadvantages** to having more online friends than real friends?

   _____

4. It is **unusual** for many people not to use technology in their daily lives.

   _____

5. Researchers have created **tests** that study whether men and women use technology differently to escape from the real world.

   _____

6. Giving up television is difficult, but **in the end**, it can have many **advantages**.

   _____

B. Read each pair of sentences. Look at the synonyms in bold. Write *G* next to the sentence that uses a more general synonym. Write *S* next to the one that uses a more specific synonym.

1. a. _G_ Second Life gives people the **opportunity** to build their dream house.

   b. _S_ Second Life gives people the **freedom** to build their dream house.

2. a. ___ People **talk** with online friends in chat rooms.

   b. ___ People **interact** with online friends in chat rooms.

3. a. ___ **I am not upset about** giving up television for a month.

   b. ___ **I don't regret** giving up television for a month.

4. a. ___ It is impossible to **explore** all the islands in Second Life.

   b. ___ It is impossible to **travel to** all the islands in Second Life.

5. a. ___ People can make real estate **sales** to residents.

   b. ___ People can make real estate **transactions** with other residents.

C. Write sentences using five pairs of synonyms from Activity A or Activity B.

1. _____

   _____

2. _____

   _____

3. _____

   _____

4. _____

   _____

5. _____

   _____

WRITING

A **summary** is a shorter version of the original text. When you write a summary, you tell the reader the main ideas of the text in your own words. Here are some things to remember when you write a summary.

A good summary:

- is in your own words (using synonyms and similar language)
- gives a basic outline of what the reading is about
- presents the main ideas in the same order as they appear in the reading
- only includes supporting **details** that are necessary to understand the main points
- is usually a paragraph in length and much shorter than the original reading

A good summary does not:

- include entire sentences that are copied from the reading
- contain any personal opinions or feelings you have about the reading
- include unnecessary **details**

A. Read the two summaries of Reading 1. Then complete the activity. Check (✓) Summary A, Summary B, or both for each statement on page 82. Compare your answers with a partner. Then discuss which summary is more effective.

Summary A

One website that has attracted millions of Internet users is Second Life. It offers an escape from real life. Users are called residents, and they create their own characters, or avatars. They buy Linden Dollars, and they can make a lot of money selling land. Users can become musicians or Olympic basketball players. Today, businesses hold meetings there. The pop group Duran Duran has given live concerts on Second Life. I think Second Life is a great way to escape reality, and I would like to try it myself.

Summary B

Second Life is a three-dimensional online environment that lets people escape reality. The online world has its own economy and currency, called the Linden Dollar. Residents use Linden Dollars to buy and sell items and land. In this world, residents have many opportunities to interact with others, at malls, clubs, and concerts, for example. Many users of Second Life escape their daily lives by exploring imaginary places and friends. Some users also choose to escape from themselves by changing their jobs, physical appearance, or nationalities. Although Second Life began as a fantasy world, today countries, businesses, and universities are also using it for real-life purposes.

1. The summary uses different words than the reading.

   Summary A _____   Summary B _____

2. The summary gives a basic outline of what the reading is about.

   Summary A _____   Summary B _____

3. The summary presents the main ideas in the same order as the reading.

   Summary A _____   Summary B _____

4. The summary includes supporting details that are necessary to understand the main points.

   Summary A _____   Summary B _____

5. The summary is a paragraph in length and much shorter than the original reading.

   Summary A _____   Summary B _____

6. The summary does not copy entire sentences from the reading.

   Summary A _____   Summary B _____

7. The summary does not contain any personal opinions or feelings.

   Summary A _____   Summary B _____

8. The summary does not include unnecessary details.

   Summary A _____   Summary B _____

B. Check (✓) the six sentences that best summarize the ideas in Reading 2. Reread the article first if you need to.

_____ 1. She called friends, read books, and did volunteer work more often.

_____ 2. The author decided to escape from TV as an experiment and eventually enjoyed the benefits of it.

_____ 3. One of her co-workers said she watches TV when her husband is gone.

_____ 4. She thought that being TV-free would help her get to know herself better.

_____ 5. She did activities she didn't have time for when she watched TV.

_____ 6. The author probably shouldn't stop watching television completely.

_____ 7. She survived a cold New England winter without a TV.

_____ 8. Now she has more free time for herself, and she is happy with her new lifestyle.

_____ 9. Eventually, her experiment turned into her everyday lifestyle.

_____ 10. Some of her friends thought she was judging them.

C. Write a summary of Reading 2 in your notebook. Use the sentences you checked in Activity B. Begin with the topic sentence. Put the ideas in the same order as they appear in the reading.

Grammar | Parallel structure

Parallel structure means using the same word form or grammatical structure to list ideas that come in a sequence. Using parallel structure makes your writing clearer and more effective. Use the conjunctions *and*, *but*, and *or* to connect parallel ideas. Look at the examples of parallel and nonparallel structures.

Parallel: Now I was <u>well read</u> *and* <u>well rested</u>.
                              adv. + ad.j   adv. + adj.

Not parallel: Now I was well read and getting more rest.

Parallel: Avatars can also attend <u>conferences</u>, <u>art shows</u>, *and* <u>concerts</u>.
                                                   noun   noun   noun

Not parallel: Avatars can also attend conferences, art shows, and there are concerts.

Parallel: Residents can <u>rent</u> *or* <u>sell</u> their land to other users.
                                        verb   verb

Not parallel: Residents can rent their land or land is sold to other users.

A. Read the sentences. Underline the parallel structures. Circle the conjunctions.

1. There are <u>games</u>, <u>shopping malls</u>, (and) <u>many kinds of stores</u> available to residents.

2. After a long day at work, they can fly to a virtual beach, meet an online friend on an imaginary planet, or build their dream house.

3. People are taking advantage of this realistic, but virtual world.

4. It was summer, the season of long walks, barbecues, and reruns.

5. I had thought that I was too tired to read after a long day at work, but not too tired to watch TV.

6. Instead of channel-surfing and watching something I would later regret, I caught up on some great films.

Tip Critical Thinking

Activity B asks you to **combine** sentences. Whether you are combining sentences, ideas, or information sources, you are putting things together to make something new. This shows that you understand information and can use it in new ways.

B. Combine each pair of sentences into one. Use *and, but,* or *or* and parallel structure.

1. Her friends were puzzled. They were supportive.

   Her friends were puzzled but supportive.

2. I didn't know what was on TV. I didn't care what was on TV.

   _____

3. People should watch TV with moderation. People should watch with a critical eye.

   _____

4. Today's online environments are more complex. They are more realistic. They are more exciting.

   _____

5. Some people decide to be a fictional creature. Some people decide to be a favorite comic-book character.

   _____

6. They can forget about their first life. They can live through their second life.

   _____

Unit Assignment | Write a summary and personal response

In this assignment, you are going to write two paragraphs. In the first paragraph, you will write a summary of Reading 2. In the second paragraph, you will write your opinion about the author's decisions and experience of living without TV. As you prepare your paragraphs, think about the Unit Question, "How has technology affected your life?" Refer to the Self-Assessment checklist on page 86. Use information from Readings 1 and 2 and your work in this unit to support your ideas.

For alternative unit assignments, see the *Q: Skills for Success Teacher's Handbook.*

PLAN AND WRITE

A. BRAINSTORM **Follows these steps to help you gather your ideas.**

1. For your summary paragraph, write the main idea of Reading 2 below. Then write down as many details as you can remember in your notebook.

    Main idea: _____

2. For your opinion paragraph, write your thoughts about the decisions the author made and her experiences in your notebook. Think about these questions as you write.

    Are there decisions she made that you agree or disagree with?

    Do you think her experience was positive or negative?

    Did anything in the reading surprise you?

Tip for Success

Before you write a summary, use the six *Wh-* questions to help you identify the main ideas in a reading: *Who? What? When? Where? Why? How?*

B. PLAN **Follow these steps to plan your paragraphs.**

1. For your summary paragraph, look at the details you wrote in Step 1 of Activity A. Circle the details that support the main idea. Cross out any smaller details that do not support the main idea. Cross out any information that expresses your opinion.

2. Write an outline for your summary paragraph.

    a. **Topic sentence:** _____

    _____

    b. **Important details:** Write the important details you circled in Step 1.

    _____

    _____

    _____

3. For your opinion paragraph, look at your thoughts from Step 2 of Activity A. Circle your best ideas.

4. Write an outline for your opinion paragraph.

    a. **Topic sentence:** Write a topic sentence that clearly expresses your opinion about Reading 2.

    _____

    _____

    b. **Reasons and examples:**

    Reason 1: _____

        Example: _____

Reason 2: _____

    Example: _____

Reason 3: _____

    Example: _____

c. **Concluding sentence:** Write a concluding sentence that restates your opinion.

_____

_____

C. `WRITE` Use your notes to write your paragraphs in your notebook. Write your summary paragraph first. Then write your opinion paragraph. Look at the Self-Assessment checklist below to guide your writing.

REVISE AND EDIT

A. `PEER REVIEW` Read a partner's paragraphs. Answer the questions and discuss them with your partner.

1. Does the summary clearly state the main ideas of Reading 2?

2. Does the summary include only the important details?

3. Does the opinion paragraph include a clear topic sentence?

4. Is the opinion paragraph supported with examples and reasons?

5. Does the opinion paragraph include a concluding sentence?

B. `REWRITE` Review the answers to the questions in Activity A. You may want to revise and rewrite your paragraphs.

C. `EDIT` Complete the Self-Assessment checklist as you prepare to write the final draft of your paragraphs. Be prepared to hand in your work or discuss it in class.

 **Your Writing Process**

For this activity, you could also use Stage 2C, *Personal Editing Checklist* in *Q Online Practice.*

SELF-ASSESSMENT		
Yes	**No**	
☐	☐	Is the punctuation correct?
☐	☐	Are all words spelled correctly?
☐	☐	Do the paragraphs include vocabulary from the unit?
☐	☐	Are parallel structures used correctly?
☐	☐	Is there a variety of synonyms used?

Circle the words you learned in this unit.

Nouns
benefit 🔑 AWL
confession
experiment 🔑
fantasy
lifestyle
limitation
occasion 🔑
transaction

Verbs
discover 🔑
explore 🔑
interact AWL
regret 🔑
survive 🔑 AWL

Adjectives
rare 🔑
realistic 🔑
social 🔑
virtual AWL

Adverb
eventually 🔑 AWL

🔑 Oxford 3000™ words
AWL Academic Word List

Check (✓) the skills you learned. If you need more work on a skill, refer to the page(s) in parentheses.

READING ⚪	I can take notes. (p. 73)
VOCABULARY ⚪	I can recognize and use synonyms. (p. 79)
WRITING ⚪	I can write a summary. (p. 81)
GRAMMAR ⚪	I can use parallel structure. (p. 83)
LEARNING OUTCOME ⚫	I can write a paragraph summarizing a reading text and an opinion paragraph in response to the text.

READING ● using a graphic organizer
VOCABULARY ● phrasal verbs
WRITING ● stating reasons and giving examples
GRAMMAR ● gerunds and infinitives

本通り　広島バス

Unit QUESTION

Why do people help each other?

PREVIEW THE UNIT

(A) **Discuss these questions with your classmates.**

Did your parents teach you to be helpful to others? Is being helpful something we learn, or is it human nature?

Are there any situations in which you don't think you should help someone? Explain.

Look at the photo. What do you think is happening?

(B) **Discuss the Unit Question above with your classmates.**

Listen to *The Q Classroom*, Track 2 on CD 2, to hear other answers.

89

C Discuss these questions in a group.

1. What are some situations in which you need help?

2. What are some situations in which other people need help?

3. Read the list of situations. Would you help? Why or why not?
   A homeless person is asking for money.
   A tourist is looking at a map on a street corner.
   A child falls down.

D Look at the pictures. Discuss these questions in a group.

1. What is happening in each picture? Where are these situations taking place?

2. Why do people help strangers in these situations?

3. Have you helped others in a similar way? Explain.

| A Question of Numbers

VOCABULARY

Here are some words from Reading 1. Read their definitions. Then complete each sentence.

> **according to** (*phr.*) as stated by someone
> **apply to** (*phr. v.*) to concern or involve someone or something
> **complex** (*adj.*) made up of several connected parts and often difficult to understand
> **end up** (*phr. v.*) to find yourself in a place or situation that you did not intend or expect
> **factor** (*n.*) something that affects a decision or situation
> **prove** (*v.*) to use facts and evidence to show that something is true
> **responsibility** (*n.*) a job or duty that you must do
> **theory** (*n.*) an idea or set of ideas that tries to explain something
> **witness** (*n.*) a person who sees something happen and who can tell other people about it later

1. _____ social psychologists, cultures have different ideas about what is good and bad behavior.

2. The police wanted to talk to the _____ who saw the thief steal the woman's purse.

3. Human behavior is _____. It is not easy to explain.

4. Scientists use a(n) _____ to explain why something happens. Then they test the idea to see whether or not it is true.

5. In some cultures, people feel it is their _____ to help their neighbors as much as they can.

6. Scientists must do experiments in order to _____ that their ideas are correct.

7. An experiment can have unexpected results. Scientists can _____ discovering something completely new or unexpected from an experiment.

8. Scientists who study people's behavior look at many different

_____ that can affect behavior, such as gender and culture.

9. Some biologists study the way our biology affects our behavior; in contrast,

social psychologists examine the way our actions _____ society.

PREVIEW READING 1

You are going to read an article from a news magazine that presents research on the *bystander effect*. The bystander effect describes how a group of ordinary people, suddenly in an emergency situation, react when help is needed.

When do you think a person is more likely to help other people? Check (✓) your answer.

☐ when he or she is alone
☐ when there are many people around

A Question of Numbers

1   You're walking down a busy city sidewalk, and you see someone in front of you fall down. What would you do? Now imagine that same situation, but you are the only other person on the sidewalk. What would you do then? **According to** social psychologists, you are more likely to help when there is no one else around. In contrast, if there are many **witnesses**, or bystanders, you might not offer help. It is even possible that no one would help the person at all. Psychologists believe this is a natural yet **complex** human reaction, which they call the *bystander effect*.

2   The bystander effect was first discovered in 1964 as a result of a very unfortunate event that happened outside Catherine Genovese's home in New York City. At three o'clock in the morning, someone attacked and murdered Genovese in front of her apartment building. The noise of the killing woke up 38 of Genovese's neighbors. All of them looked out of their windows to see what was happening. However, not one of those 38 witnesses did anything to help. No one reported the murder to the police. The whole nation was shocked by the news the next day, and psychologists had no answers to explain why these people didn't help.

3   Newspapers called the 38 witnesses selfish and uncaring, but social psychologists John Darley and Bibb Latane had a different **theory**. They believed that a large number of witnesses actually *decreased* the chances that any individual would help. If only one person witnesses a murder, he or she will feel fully responsible for calling the police. If there are two witnesses, each person might feel only half responsible. Now imagine there are many witnesses, as in the Genovese case. Darley and Latane pointed out that each person felt only a small amount of **responsibility**, so each did nothing. The reason they didn't help was not that they were uncaring or selfish people. There were just too many of them.

4   Darley and Latane knew they had to **prove** their theory scientifically, so they set up an experiment with college students to test it. They divided the students into three groups. They took each student to a small building. They put him or her in a room with a TV screen that showed another person in a different room in the building; then they left. Students in the first group thought that they were alone in the building. Students in the second group thought that there was one other person in the building. Students in the third group thought that there were four other people in the building. As part of the experiment, the person on the TV screen pretended[1] to become ill and called out for help. In the first group, where students believed

---

[1] **pretend:** to behave as if something is true or real, when it is not

The bystander effect is common on busy city streets.

they were the only people in the building, 85 percent went to get help for the person. In the second group, only 62 percent tried to help. In the third group, only 31 percent tried to help. The results supported Darley and Latane's theory. They figured out that having more witnesses did not mean that help was more likely. In fact, the opposite was true.

5   Social psychologists believe the bystander effect can **apply to** a number of everyday situations. For example, on a busy sidewalk, you might not give money to a homeless man (or help someone who falls down). On a crowded subway, you may not give up your seat to an elderly person. On the highway, you might choose not to stop and help someone change a flat tire. In these situations, you—and the other bystanders—feel less responsible because so many people are around to help, so no one **ends up** helping at all.

6   The bystander effect is one of the many **factors** that influence a person's decision to help out a stranger in need. Some people might naturally feel more desire to help. Some cultures might put more importance on helping strangers than others do. Some cities and towns could be designed to be more friendly than others. However, psychologists know that humans are naturally influenced by the presence of others around them even if they are not aware of it.

MAIN IDEAS

Read the statements. Write *T* (true) or *F* (false) according to the reading.

_____ 1. The bystander effect is a natural human reaction that occurs in situations in which help is needed.

_____ 2. Social psychologists studied the bystander effect before the murder of Catherine Genovese.

_____ 3. Darley and Latane's experiment showed that having more witnesses meant that help was less likely.

_____ 4. Darley and Latane studied the bystander effect by watching how people behave in everyday situations.

_____ 5. The bystander effect is one of the factors that influence people's decision to help others.

DETAILS

Circle the answer that best completes each statement.

1. Catherine Genovese's murder occurred ____.
   a. outside New York City
   b. in her apartment
   c. in front of her apartment building

2. When only one person witnesses a crime, he or she will feel ____ for calling the police.
   a. not responsible
   b. partly responsible
   c. fully responsible

3. Darley and Latane's experiment divided college students into ____ different groups.
   a. two
   b. three
   c. four

4. In Darley and Latane's experiment, ____ of the students who thought they were alone went to get help for the victim.
   a. 85 percent
   b. 62 percent
   c. 31 percent

5. Helping strangers may be more important in some ____.
   a. cities
   b. cultures
   c. psychologists

 **WHAT DO YOU THINK?**

Discuss the questions in a group. Then choose one question and write five to eight sentences in response.

1. Have you ever *not* helped someone who needed help? Why or why not? What factors might make someone choose not to help a stranger?

2. In general, which people do you think are more helpful to strangers in need: people who live in cities or people who live in small towns? Why?

3. The author of "A Question of Numbers" writes that "some cultures might put more importance on helping strangers than others do." Do you think that a person's culture can be a factor in making him or her a more helpful person? Why or why not?

| Reading Skill | Using a graphic organizer | |

Graphic organizers represent ideas with images, such as diagrams, charts, tables, and timelines. You can use graphic organizers to help you see connections between ideas or remember the main points of a text or parts of a text. Using graphic organizers can help you review a text you have read in preparation for class or a test.

The flowchart below organizes the main points of a scientific article.

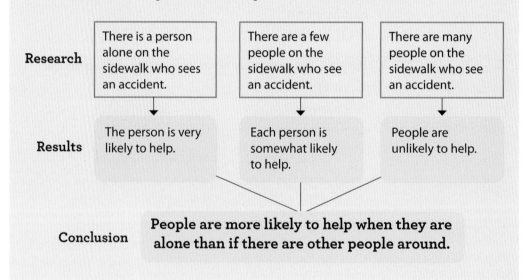

Activity A uses a
graphic organizer
to **illustrate** the
ideas of a reading.
When you illustrate,
you make a picture
of information or
ideas. This is a good
way to understand
material and to
review for a test.

A. With a partner, look at a student's graphic organizer for Paragraph 4 of Reading 1. Then discuss the questions.

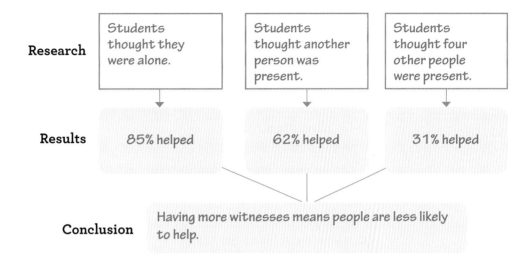

Research

| Students thought they were alone. | Students thought another person was present. | Students thought four other people were present. |

Results

85% helped · 62% helped · 31% helped

Conclusion · Having more witnesses means people are less likely to help.

Tip for Success

Looking for patterns
of organization in
a text will help you
understand what
the writer wants to
say about the topic.

1. How does the flowchart organize information from the reading?

2. Look at the labels on the left. Are these words from the reading or from the student who made the graphic organizer?

3. Does the graphic organizer make the information easier to understand?

B. Work with a partner. Use the flowchart from Activity A. Complete the summary of Paragraph 4 of Reading 1.

Darley and Latane researched the bystander effect using

_____ groups of students in different situations. When
　　　　(1)

students thought they were _____, 85 percent tried
　　　　　　　　　　　　　　(2)

to help someone in need. When they thought one other student was

present, _____ tried to help. Finally, only 31 percent
　　　　(3)

helped when students thought _____ other bystanders
　　　　　　　　　　　　　(4)

were present. Based on these results, Darley and Latane concluded that

_____ .
　　　　　　　　　(5)

READING 2 | The Biology of Altruism

VOCABULARY

Here are some words and phrases from Reading 2. Read the sentences.
Circle the answer that best matches the meaning of each bold word or
phrase. Then compare your answers with a partner.

1. The man who saved the child's life received a medal of honor from the city
   for his **altruistic** act.
   a. worried about what others will think of you
   b. caring about others with no advantage for yourself
   c. shy and not very sociable

2. Each **subject** in the medical study was paid fifty dollars for answering
   questions about his or her health.
   a. a person who works in hospitals
   b. a person who is part of an experiment
   c. a person who doesn't have enough money

3. The researcher could **barely** hear anything because there was so much
   noise coming from outside.
   a. hardly; almost not
   b. completely
   c. often

4. Some scientists **hypothesize** that natural instincts and how we are raised
   have an equal effect on how helpful we are. Others believe one has more
   influence than the other.
   a. state that something is definitely true
   b. suggest a possible explanation
   c. disagree strongly with someone

5. Designing an experiment well can **lead to** useful results. In contrast, a
   poorly designed experiment can result in unreliable information.
   a. control
   b. end
   c. cause

6. Watching people on a crowded sidewalk can **bring about** a better
   understanding of how the bystander effect works in real life.
   a. cause
   b. destroy something
   c. improve the look of something

7. Health-care workers are usually **compassionate** people—they want to help others in need.

   a. caring about other people's feelings

   b. having enough money

   c. taking more than your fair share

8. All scientists **rely on** experiments to test whether their ideas are true or false. They never guess that an idea is right before testing it.

   a. use occasionally

   b. need and depend on

   c. think about

9. The results of the **initial** study were correct because every study after it showed the same conclusions.

   a. last in a series

   b. something that is at the beginning; first

   c. of little importance

PREVIEW READING 2

You are going to read an article from a science journal that presents research on how the brain can influence a person's decision to help strangers.

Read the first and last paragraphs. Why do you think people want to help strangers? Check (✓) your answer(s).

☐ It makes them feel good.

☐ It helps people survive.

☐ They feel they have to.

☐ They want something in return.

☐ It makes them feel important.

☐ It is polite.

CD 2
Track 4   **Read the article.**

The Biology of Altruism

1   Scientific evidence suggests that humans have a biological desire to help others, including strangers. **Altruistic** behavior towards strangers is uniquely human and observed at a very young age. Dr. Felix Warneken and Dr. Michael Tomasello of Germany's Max Planck Institute for Evolutionary Anthropology have shown that children as young as 18 months want to help strangers. When their 18-month-old **subjects** saw a stranger throw a pencil on the floor, none of them picked it up. However, when the same subjects saw someone "accidentally" drop a pencil, nearly all the children picked it up in the first ten seconds. Says Dr. Warneken, "The results were astonishing because these children are so young. They still wear diapers and are **barely** able to use language, but they already show helping behavior." Because altruistic behavior appears in children so young, Dr. Warneken and other scientists **hypothesize** that the human brain is designed to be altruistic.

Mirror Neurons

2   By using brain scans[1], neuroscientists are making new discoveries about the biology of the human brain. The recent discovery of mirror neurons in humans **leads to** scientists' belief that the brain can influence altruistic behavior. Mirror neurons are ordinary brain cells located throughout the brain. They "light up" when a person is performing an action or observing someone else doing a similar action. Mirror neurons make us cry when we see someone else

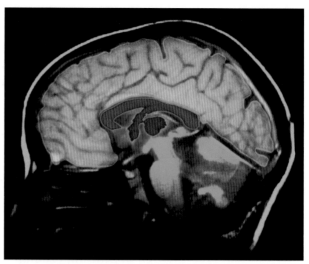

Brain scans like this one help scientists see the brain in action.

cry or smile when someone smiles at us. Our mirror neurons actually feel what they feel. They cry and smile along with them.

3   How, then, can mirror neurons **bring about** altruistic behavior? By helping us feel what others feel, mirror neurons naturally make us feel **compassionate**. They allow us to put ourselves in someone else's situation; without them, we would not understand or care about other people's emotions. Would we help hurricane victims[2]? Give money to the poor? Save lives? Probably not, says Marco Iacoboni, a leading neuroscientist: "We are good because our biology drives us[3] to be good." In other words, mirror neurons seem to prepare us to be altruistic.

Neuroeconomics

4   Neuroeconomist Bill Harbaugh and his team at the University of Oregon study the biology of altruism. They look specifically at

---

[1] **brain scan:** an image of the brain taken by a special machine

[2] **victim:** a person harmed or killed as a result of a crime or accident

[3] **drive:** to motivate, or cause someone to act in a particular way

neuroeconomics, or the connection between the brain and economic decisions. In one of their experiments, the researchers tried seeing if people's donations to charity[4] were affected by neurons. Nineteen women were given $100 to play a charity game on the computer. They could choose to donate or not to a charity, each decision leading to other situations where they could gain or lose money. At the end of the game, the subjects were able to keep all the money that was left in their accounts.

5   As the subjects played the game, the scientists scanned their brains. They looked at the brain's "pleasure center," which controls how good people feel. When most subjects donated money to a charity, their pleasure centers lit up on the brain scan. Some even lit up when the subjects were taxed on their donation. Both results suggest that the brain's pleasure center is rewarded for altruistic acts. In addition, the more people donated, the more their pleasure centers lit up. For some, the pleasure center lit up more when the computer gave the charity extra money than when they received extra money to keep for themselves. The scientists point out that this was "the first neural evidence for … pure altruism," meaning that altruism may indeed have a biological connection.

Unanswered Questions

6   Why would our brains be biologically prepared to help others? What benefit does it have for each of us and for human beings as a whole? One popular scientific theory suggests that being natural helpers improves our chances of survival. Humans are social creatures, dependent on family, friends, governments, and strangers. Babies need food to survive, but they also need someone there to feed them. Larger social groups also **rely on** our help, such as when we pay taxes or donate money to charities. Without a "helping brain," humans would have a much harder time trying to survive.

7   The study of the biology of altruism still has a long way to go, however. Many questions have grown out of these **initial** studies. For instance, if humans are born with a "helping" brain, why do we also have the ability to hurt others? Why are some of us more altruistic than others? How much control does the brain have on altruistic behavior? How much influence does society have? As technology advances, scientists hope to find answers to these questions and increase our understanding of ourselves.

---

[4] **charity:** an organization set up to help people in need

MAIN IDEAS

Circle the answer to each question.

1. What is the main idea of the reading?
   a. Research suggests that the brain influences our desire to help others.
   b. Humans survive because they are natural helpers.
   c. Children as young as 18 months have the desire to help strangers.

2. Which of the following is <u>not</u> true about mirror neurons?
   a. They light up when a person is doing something.
   b. They make us feel compassionate towards others.
   c. They are different from ordinary brain cells.

3. What is neuroeconomics?
   a. the study of how the brain makes decisions about money
   b. the study of how the brain controls donations to charities
   c. the study of how the brain's pleasure center works

4. What did Dr. Harbaugh's study reveal about neuroeconomics?
   a. Some people get pleasure from being taxed on donations.
   b. The brain's pleasure center is not rewarded for altruistic acts.
   c. Donating money does not light up the brain's pleasure center.

5. Why might people be born with a "helping brain"?
   a. Human babies need parents to feed them.
   b. It improves people's chances of survival.
   c. People have to live and work with others.

DETAILS

Read the statements. Write *T* (true) or *F* (false). Then correct each false statement to make it true.

_____ 1. When 18-month-old subjects saw a stranger throw a pencil on the floor, they picked it up immediately.

_____ 2. Very young children show altruistic behavior.

_____ 3. Scientists believe that the brain can influence human behavior.

_____ 4. Scientists have known about mirror neurons for hundreds of years.

_____ 5. Without mirror neurons, we would not understand or care about other people's emotions.

_____ **6.** In Bill Harbaugh's experiments, women were given $1,000 to play a charity game.

_____ **7.** The subjects' memory centers lit up when they donated money.

 ## WHAT DO YOU THINK?

A. Discuss the questions in a group.

1. How altruistic do you think you are? Give examples to support your opinion.

2. Why do you think some people are more altruistic than others?

B. Think about both Reading 1 and Reading 2 as you discuss the questions. Then choose one question and write five to eight sentences in response.

1. What do you think has more influence on our decision to help other people: the presence of others or human nature?

2. Can a person's own life experiences make him or her a more helpful person? Explain, using examples from your own observations and experiences.

Vocabulary Skill | **Phrasal verbs**

A **phrasal verb** is a combination of a verb and a particle. Particles are usually prepositions, such as *up*, *on*, *in*, *down*, and *over*. When they are used in a phrasal verb, however, they can change the meaning of the verb.

Compare these pairs of sentences.

> The scientist was finished with his research, so he **ended** the experiments.
> He tried to help the old man find the address, but he **ended up** taking him home.
>
> Bob and Al like to **watch** ice hockey on the weekends.
> **Watch out** for that rock! It looks as if it's going to fall!

The phrasal verb *end up* has a different meaning from the verb *end*.

> end   →   to finish
> end up   →   to be in a situation after a series of events

The phrasal verb *watch out* has a different meaning from the verb *watch*.

> watch   →   to look carefully or with interest at something
> watch out   →   to be careful about something

A. These phrasal verbs appear in the readings in this unit. Match each phrasal verb with its definition. Look back at the readings or use your dictionary to help you.

_____ 1. set up (Reading 1, Paragraph 4)

_____ 2. call out (Reading 1, Paragraph 4)

_____ 3. figure out (Reading 1, Paragraph 4)

_____ 4. help out (Reading 1, Paragraph 6)

_____ 5. point out (Reading 2, Paragraph 5)

_____ 6. grow out of (Reading 2, Paragraph 7)

a. to tell or show something that people didn't know or think about

b. to develop from

c. to find an answer to something or to understand

d. to prepare something

e. to assist somebody

f. to say something loudly or shout in order to attract attention

B. Complete this short article wth phrasal verbs from Activity A.

Darley and Latane _____ experiments with college
                          (1)
students to _____ why no bystanders reacted to the murder
                   (2)
of Catherine Genovese. Their study helped _____ new
                                                  (3)
information that they didn't expect. They discovered that the presence

of more people at a scene makes people feel less responsible. The study

also showed that people in groups don't react to a problem if nobody

else acts or looks concerned. They assume that nothing is wrong, even if

they hear someone _____ for help. There have been other
                         (4)
experiments since Darley and Latane's findings. Probably even more

studies will _____ their research because psychologists are
                 (5)
very interested in knowing more about what other factors affect people's

decisions to _____ those in need.
                 (6)

WRITING

Writers state **reasons** to explain why something happens. Reasons can explain why people act or do things in a certain way or why things happen. Writers support their reasons with **examples**. Examples can be specific situations or personal observations that writers give to make their reasons clearer.

> **Topic sentence:** Some people don't know their neighbors very well.
>
> **Reason 1:** They don't see each other often enough.
> **Example:** They work so much that they are rarely at home during the day.
> **Example:** They prefer not to spend much time outside.
>
> **Reason 2:** They make wrong assumptions about their neighbors.
> **Example:** They think their neighbors are unfriendly when in fact they are really just shy.
> **Example:** They assume their neighbors are not interested in being friends.

There are certain phrases that signal examples, such as:

> For example,
> For instance,

Stating reasons with *because*

Because is often used to show reasons why something happens or is true. When *because* is at the beginning of a sentence, a comma is put before the second subject-verb combination.

>   reason   second subject-verb combination
> Because they don't feel safe themselves, they don't think they can help someone else.

When *because* is in the middle of a sentence, no comma is used.

>   reason
> People may not help because they don't feel safe.

Tip for Success

Why questions appear on many tests. The test is asking you to state reasons. These are some words that signal *why* questions:

Explain why …

Give reasons for …

Discuss the causes of …

A. Read the paragraphs. Put a check mark (✓) next to the reasons and underline examples. Then write them in the outline that follows.

Why We Don't Help

There are a number of reasons why someone might not help a stranger in need. First of all, we might be too busy to help. For example, people might not stop to help a stranded driver on the side of the road because they are in a hurry to get to work. Another reason people may not help is because they don't feel safe. For instance, when people hear a stranger scream in the middle of the night, they might be too scared to help out. Since they don't feel safe themselves, they don't think they can help someone else. Finally, we might not help others because we assume they can help themselves. For example, if someone on the sidewalk seems to be lost, people think that he or she can find the necessary information without help.

Overall, the decision not to help is very complex. Time, safety, and thinking people can help themselves are just three of many reasons a person chooses not to help others.

1. **Topic sentence:**

   There are a number of reasons why someone might not help a stranger in need.

2. **Reasons and examples:**

   Reason 1: _too busy to help_

   Example: _don't stop for stranded driver; in hurry to get to work_

   Reason 2: _____

   Example: _____

   Reason 3: _____

   Example: _____

3. **Concluding sentence:** _____

   _____

B. Read the sentences. Underline the reasons. Add commas if needed.

1. <u>Because the witnesses didn't feel responsible</u>, they did nothing to help.

2. Because our brains have mirror neurons we can feel what others feel.

3. The scientists performed an experiment because they wanted to prove their theory.

4. Altruistic behavior is complex because many factors are involved.

5. People might help others because it improves their chances of survival.

6. Because the street was so busy no one noticed the man.

Grammar Gerunds and infinitives

A **gerund** is the base form of a **verb** + **ing**. Gerunds function as nouns in a sentence. A gerund can be one word (*running, eating, living*) or part of a phrase (*running outdoors, eating healthily, living in a big city*).

Gerunds as subjects

A gerund or **gerund phrase** can be the subject of a sentence. A gerund subject always takes a singular verb.

> **Helping** <u>is</u> easier when we feel safe.
> **Being altruistic** <u>means</u> helping others without expecting anything in return.

Gerunds after verbs

Gerunds follow certain verbs. Here are some of the verbs that gerunds follow:

avoid	discuss	enjoy	go	quit
consider	dislike	finish	practice	suggest

An **infinitive** is *to* + **the base form** of a verb. Infinitives can also function as nouns in sentences.

> They wanted **to donate** money.

Infinitives after verbs

Infinitives follow certain verbs. Here are some of the verbs infinitives follow:

agree	decide	hope	plan	wait
appear	forget	learn	seem	want

A. Complete each sentence with a gerund phrase. Use the words in parentheses.

1. ___Studying social psychology___ (study/social psychology) is very interesting.

2. _____ (understand/human behavior) is not always easy.

3. _____ (help/other people) is part of human nature.

4. _____ (donate/money) is an example of altruistic behavior.

5. _____ (use/brain scans) has helped scientists better understand human behavior.

6. _____ (live/in a big city) can be stressful sometimes.

B. Complete each sentence with a verb + a gerund.

1. I wanted to be healthier, but I really _____ *dislike exercising* _____ (dislike/exercise).

2. If you have heart problems, you should _____ (quit/eat) salty foods.

3. Monica and Rodrigo _____ (consider/move) to Chicago, but they decided to stay in Miami.

4. We should _____ (avoid/buy) a big car. Gasoline is too expensive.

5. In our next class, we are going to _____ (discuss/write) paragraphs.

6. After Margo _____ (finish/eat) dinner, she read the newspaper.

C. Complete each sentence with a gerund or an infinitive.

1. I hope _____ *to go* _____ (go) to Australia someday.

2. Yuri wants _____ (visit) his friend in Seoul next fall.

3. You should practice _____ (speak) Spanish every day if you want to become fluent.

4. My neighbor agreed _____ (help) me move into my new apartment.

5. Do you enjoy _____ (play) soccer?

6. Vanessa goes _____ (swim) every morning with her daughter.

In this assignment, you are going to write a paragraph with reasons and examples. As you prepare your paragraph, think about the Unit Question, "Why do people help each other?" Refer to the Self-Assessment checklist on page 110. Use information from Readings 1 and 2 and your work in this unit to support your ideas.

For alternative unit assignments, see the *Q: Skills for Success Teacher's Handbook*.

PLAN AND WRITE

A. **BRAINSTORM** In a group, brainstorm reasons other than than the ones in the readings that might affect a person's decision to help others. Write your ideas in your notebook.

B. **PLAN** Follow these steps as you plan your paragraph.

1. Look at your notes from Activity A. Circle the reasons you want to include in your paragraph. Then think of examples to support these reasons.

2. Think about the readings in this unit. Is there any information from them that can help support your ideas?

3. Write an outline for your paragraph.

   a. **Topic sentence:** _____

   _____

   b. **Reasons and examples:**

   Reason 1: _____

   _____

       Example: _____

   _____

   Reason 2: _____

   _____

       Example: _____

   _____

   Reason 3: _____

   _____

Example: _____

_____

c. **Concluding sentence:** _____

_____

C. WRITE Write your paragraph in your notebook. Use your outline from Activity B. Use *because* when you state some of your reasons. Look at the Self-Assessment checklist below to guide your writing.

REVISE AND EDIT

A. PEER REVIEW Read a partner's paragraph. Answer the questions and discuss them with your partner.

1. Does the paragraph have a clear topic sentence? Underline it.

2. Do the reasons support the topic sentence?

3. Are examples given to support the reasons?

B. REWRITE Review the answers to the questions in Activity A. You may want to revise and rewrite your paragraph.

C. EDIT Complete the Self-Assessment checklist as you prepare to write the final draft of your paragraph. Be prepared to hand in your work or discuss it in class.

SELF-ASSESSMENT		
Yes	No	
☐	☐	Is the punctuation correct?
☐	☐	Are all words spelled correctly?
☐	☐	Does the paragraph include vocabulary from the unit?
☐	☐	Does the paragraph include a topic sentence with reasons that support it?
☐	☐	Does the paragraph contain examples to support reasons?
☐	☐	Is *because* used correctly to state reasons? Are commas used if necessary?
☐	☐	Does the paragraph use phrasal verbs from the unit? Are they used correctly?
☐	☐	Do gerunds end in *-ing*?
☐	☐	Are all gerund subjects followed by a singular verb?

Circle the words you learned in this unit.

Nouns
factor 🔑 AWL
responsibility 🔑
subject 🔑
theory 🔑 AWL
witness 🔑

Verbs
apply (to) 🔑
hypothesize AWL
lead (to) 🔑
prove 🔑
rely (on) 🔑 AWL

Adjectives
altruistic
compassionate
complex 🔑 AWL
initial 🔑 AWL

Adverb
barely 🔑

Phrasal Verbs
bring about
call out

end up
figure out
grow out of
help out
point out
set up
watch out

Phrase
according to 🔑

🔑 Oxford 3000™ words
AWL Academic Word List

Check (✓) the skills you learned. If you need more work on a skill, refer to the page(s) in parentheses.

READING	●	I can use a graphic organizer. (p. 96)
VOCABULARY	●	I can use phrasal verbs. (p. 103)
WRITING	●	I can state reasons and give examples. (p. 105)
GRAMMAR	●	I can use gerunds and infinitives. (p. 107)
LEARNING OUTCOME	●	I can write a paragraph about why people help others using reasons and examples.

READING ● distinguishing facts from opinions
VOCABULARY ● suffixes
WRITING ● writing a letter to the editor
GRAMMAR ● compound sentences

Unit QUESTION

Does advertising help or harm us?

PREVIEW THE UNIT

Ⓐ Discuss these questions with your classmates.

What things have you bought because of an advertisement?

Has an advertisement ever helped you in some way? What kind of ad was it? How did it help you?

Look at the photo. Where are these signs? Why are they there?

Ⓑ Discuss the Unit Question above with your classmates.

Listen to *The Q Classroom*, Track 5 on CD 2, to hear other answers.

113

C Discuss these questions in a group.

1. Where do you typically see advertisements?

2. Look at the photos below. Where do you think you might see advertisements like the ones in the photos?

Tip Critical Thinking

Activity D asks you to separate the advertisements into **categories** according to purpose. **Categorizing** things helps you notice the way things are similar or different.

D Check (✓) the purpose of each advertisement in Activity C.

	to provide information	to provide help	to sell something
Advertisement 1	☐	☐	☐
Advertisement 2	☐	☐	☐
Advertisement 3	☐	☐	☐
Advertisement 4	☐	☐	☐

READING 1 | Happiness Is in the Shoes You Wear

VOCABULARY

Here are some words and phrases from Reading 1. Read their definitions. Then complete each sentence.

> **consequence** (*n.*) a result or effect of something
>
> **imply** (*v.*) to suggest something in an indirect way
>
> **means to an end** (*idm.*) an action that is not important in itself, but is a way of achieving something else
>
> **possession** (*n.*) something that you own
>
> **recent** (*adj.*) happened a short time ago
>
> **relationship** (*n.*) a friendly or emotional connection between two people
>
> **trivial** (*adj.*) of little importance
>
> **tune out** (*phr. v.*) to stop listening to or to ignore
>
> **unpredictable** (*adj.*) changing often so that you don't know what to expect

1. The weather report earlier this week said it was going to be sunny this weekend, but the most _____ report said it was going to rain.

2. The weather in Boston is _____. It can be warm and sunny one day and then cold and rainy the next.

3. Karen has a good _____ with her mother. They talk on the phone every day and enjoy spending time together.

4. Although advertisements don't actually say this, many of them _____ that you'll be happier, more successful, more beautiful, etc., if you buy the product.

5. Working as an assistant is just a(n) _____. Tina hopes she will be promoted to a higher position in a few years.

6. When Leo works, he often listens to music because it helps him _____ the other noise at the office.

7. We can't waste time during the meeting discussing _____ things. We have many important issues to discuss today.

8. There was a big snowstorm yesterday, and as a(n) _____, many schools and businesses were closed for the day.

9. Maria is very wealthy, but she says her most valued _____ is the photograph of her family.

What makes people happy?

PREVIEW READING 1

You are going to read an article from a news magazine. It discusses how advertising tries to make us believe that we can achieve happiness by buying products.

Read the first sentence of each paragraph. What is the author's opinion about this practice? Have you seen any ads that you think try to do this? If yes, what were the ads for? Write your ideas.

_____

_____

_____

Happiness Is in the Shoes You Wear

1   A **recent** ad for shoes asks, "When was the last time you felt this comfortable in a **relationship**?" After all, it is easier to love a product than a person. Relationships with human beings can be messy and **unpredictable**. Our shoes never ask us to wash the dishes or tell us we're getting fat.

2   This ad is meant to be funny. I suppose it might seem amusing or, at worst, tasteless. As someone who has studied ads for a long time, however, I see it as part of a pattern: just one example of many ads that state or **imply** that products are more important than people. Ads have always promised us a better relationship via a product: *buy this and you will be loved*. But more recently they have gone beyond that to promise us a relationship with the product itself: *buy this and it will love you*. The product is not so much the **means to an end**, as the end itself.

Diamonds Are Forever

3   We are surrounded by hundreds, thousands of messages every day that connect our deepest emotions to products, that turn people into objects and make our most heartfelt moments and relationships unimportant. Every emotion is used to sell us something. Our wish to protect our children forces us to buy an expensive car. A long marriage simply provides the occasion for a diamond necklace. A tearful reunion between a father and his daughter is used to sell us a phone system. Everything in the world—nature, animals, people—is just one more item to be consumed or to be used to sell us something.

4   The problem with advertising isn't that it creates artificial needs, but that it takes advantage[1] of our very real and human desires. Most of us want committed relationships that will last. We are not stupid: We know that buying a certain brand of cereal won't bring us one inch closer to that goal. But we are surrounded by advertising that connects our needs with products. Advertising promises us that *things* will deliver something that they never can.

5   Most people feel that advertising is not something to take seriously. Although advertising has been studied more carefully in recent years than ever before, just about everyone still feels free from its influence. What I hear more than anything else at my lectures is: "I don't pay attention to ads ... I just **tune** them **out** ... they have no effect on me." I hear this most from people wearing clothes with logos[2]. In truth, we are all influenced. There is no way to tune out this much information, especially when it is designed to break through the "tuning out" process. As advertising critic Sut Jhally put it, "To not be influenced by advertising would be to live outside of culture. No human being lives outside of culture." Much of advertising's power comes from this belief that it does not affect us.

---

[1] **to take advantage of:** to make unfair use of somebody or somebody's kindness in order to get what you want
[2] **logo:** a symbol used as an advertisement by a company

Because we think advertising is **trivial**, we are less critical than we might otherwise be. But while we're laughing, the commercial does its work.

6 Taken individually, ads are silly, sometimes funny, certainly nothing to worry about. But taken all together, they can cause us to distrust other people and harm relationships. Ads portray our real lives as dull and ordinary, commitment to human beings as something to be avoided. Because this kind of message appears everywhere, we learn from childhood that it is safer to make a commitment to a product than to a person, easier to be loyal to a brand. Many end up feeling attached to material objects yet deeply distrustful of other human beings.

7 In the world of advertising, relationships grow cold, people grow old, children grow up and move away—but **possessions** stay with us and never change. But possessions can't make us happy or loved or less alone or safe. If we believe they can, we are doomed to disappointment. No matter how much we love them, they will never love us back.

8 Advertising creates a world view that is based upon distrust, dissatisfaction, and desire. Advertisers aren't evil. They are just doing their job, which is to sell a product; but the **consequences** are often harmful. The story that advertising tells is that the way to be happy, to find satisfaction, is through the consumption of material objects.

MAIN IDEAS

Read the sentences. Check (✓) the main ideas of the article.

____ 1. Advertisements imply that things are more important than people.

____ 2. Advertising connects products to human emotions to sell things.

____ 3. Most people can tune out advertising.

____ 4. The way to be happy is through buying things.

____ 5. Ads try to convince us that products can offer us what relationships can't.

DETAILS

Read the statements. Write *T* (true) or *F* (false). Then correct each false statement to make it true according to the article.

____ 1. Ads have always made a promise: *buy this and you'll be wealthy.*

____ 2. Our wish to protect our children can make us buy an expensive car.

____ 3. A tearful reunion between a father and daughter is used to sell a diamond necklace.

____ 4. Most people believe that advertising is not something to take seriously.

____ 5. People say that they pay close attention to ads and watch them closely.

____ 6. Because we think ads are trivial, we are more critical of them.

WHAT DO YOU THINK?

Discuss the questions in a group. Then choose one question and write five to eight sentences in response.

1. Do you believe that things can make you happy? Have you ever received something that made you very happy? How long did the happiness last?

2. Have you ever felt influenced to buy something because of an ad? What about the ad made you want to buy this item?

| Reading Skill | Distinguishing facts from opinions | |

A **fact** is a statement that is true and can be proven true. An **opinion** usually expresses a personal judgment or gives a position about something. Good readers can quickly tell whether a statement is a fact or an opinion. Look at these two statements.

> My parents have been married for 25 years. (fact)
> Relationships with human beings are messy and unpredictable. (opinion)

The first statement is a fact. We can find the date of their marriage and prove it. The second statement is an opinion. It cannot be proven, and people could have a different opinion about relationships from the writer's. In addition, adjectives such as *messy* and *unpredictable* indicate the writer's opinion. Here are two more examples.

> Class starts at 7:30 a.m. (fact)
> My classes are difficult. (opinion)

A. Read the statements. Write *F* (fact) or *O* (opinion).

____ 1. Ads are silly, sometimes trivial.

____ 2. There were eight ads for appliances in a recent news magazine.

____ 3. Advertising can be ignored easily.

____ 4. During every half-hour television show, there are 12 minutes of commercial advertising.

____ 5. The ads during the sports program were very funny.

____ 6. Ads create a dangerous climate of distrust.

B. Read the sentences. Underline the part of each sentence that makes it an opinion.

1. People are always influenced by ads.

2. Taken individually, ads are silly, sometimes funny, but certainly nothing to worry about.

3. My favorite ad is the one showing the family in the beautiful new car.

4. That was the most ridiculous ad I have ever seen.

5. The consequences of ads are harmful.

READING 2 | **In Defense of Advertising**

VOCABULARY

Here are some words from Reading 2. Read the sentences. Then write each bold word next to the correct definition on page 121.

1. Some food companies use some of their profits to **support** programs for seriously ill children.

2. This is a useful website, but I can't stand all of the pop-up ads. They're so **annoying**!

3. Radio **broadcasting** brings music, news, and other programs to the public.

4. The young girl's performance on the television show gave her the **exposure** she needed to become a well-known singer.

5. All of the ads on the fence **surrounding** the baseball field are for food products that are sold there.

6. There is always a guest speaker at the college's **annual** graduation dinner. This year, it will be the mayor!

7. The children were bored at dinner, so we turned on the TV to **entertain** them.

8. That was a very **memorable** movie. After all these years, I still remember the ending very clearly.

9. Many food companies make **donations** of their products to organizations that feed the hungry.

a. _____ (*adj.*) making you feel slightly angry

b. _____ (*adj.*) happening or done once a year

c. _____ (*n.*) attention from newspapers, television, or other media

d. _____ (*n.*) sound or pictures that are sent by radio or television

e. _____ (*n.*) money or things that are given to an organization

f. _____ (*v.*) to interest and amuse someone

g. _____ (*v.*) to give or provide someone or something with assistance and money

h. _____ (*adj.*) being or going around someone or something

i. _____ (*adj.*) easy to remember because it is special in some way

PREVIEW READING 2

This is an article based on a Canadian radio show. It gives us a less common opinion of advertising—it points out ways advertising benefits people.

Read the first and last paragraphs of the article. What are some ways that advertising can be helpful to people?

 CD 2 Track 7   **Read the article.**

In Defense of Advertising

1   How often do we hear comments such as these: "I hate advertising," or "There's too much advertising in the world!" In the 21st century, it seems that advertising is everywhere we look. We see it along highways, in trains, buses, even in taxicabs, as well as on the Internet and on TV. It's hard to escape advertising. But do we really want to? Actually, when you think about it, advertising provides us with quite a few benefits.

2   First, advertising gives us information that we need. For instance, if you want to buy a new appliance or a new car, you can look for the best "deals" in ads that appear in

newspapers, in magazines, on television, or even on the radio. These ads give you details about the product and help you find out where you can get the best price for something. You don't actually have to go to lots of different stores. So, in this way, advertising provides a service for the consumer.

3 Besides providing information, advertising also **supports** the arts, including television and movies. It may be **annoying** to sit through commercials during your favorite TV show, but the advertisers have paid for its production. This, in turn, pays the actors for their work. Even public **broadcasting** has supporters. The companies' names appear at the beginning or end of the shows. Without their support, there would be more hours of pledge drives[1] asking you, the consumer, for more money. As for movies, we find out about them through ads, and we decide which ones we want to see based on ads for them. Additionally, many performing artists, such as actors and musicians, get their starts from writing or appearing in commercials or print advertisements. It's a way for them to get both experience and **exposure**.

4 And what about advertising and sports? There are hundreds of large banners **surrounding** sports stadiums, and hundreds, thousands, even millions of people notice them. Professional sports depend on advertising to pay for the fields, the equipment, and yes, even the salaries of professional athletes. Think about the Super Bowl in the United States. Everyone looks forward to this **annual** event, even those who do not like football, because the commercials are known to be the best of the year. Companies pay as much as a million dollars for 60 seconds of advertising time during this event, so a lot of effort goes into these commercials. As a result, viewers want to watch the commercials almost as much as the sports.

5 When we're not out shopping or being **entertained**, many of us enjoy "surfing" the Web. Whenever you open a page in Google or go on a social networking site, such as Facebook, there are dozens of ads. These ads help pay for the services that the websites provide. Without the advertising, the websites could not provide those services. They would not have the money to continue.

6 There has always been a "good" side to advertising in the form of public service announcements (PSAs). These are advertisements that provide people with information about issues like diseases or medical problems, as well as public health and safety. The commercials are often very creative and informative. They provide viewers with the information they need in a **memorable** way. Various companies pay for the PSAs, and advertising agencies make **donations** of their time and expertise to produce them.

7 It would be a much duller, certainly less colorful world without advertising. Think of all of the ways that advertising improves our world. The next time you look at that clothing catalog, think of all of the creativity and work that went into making it. From clothing designers, photographers, models and artists, to paper company workers and store employees—thousands of people worked to help produce that catalog. And when you watch your favorite TV show, remember that the commercials were partly responsible for what you've just watched and enjoyed. We may wish that commercials and advertisements weren't necessary at all, but, for the most part, we are all content to have them as part of our lives.

---

[1] **pledge drive:** an effort by a group of people to raise money, which people promise to pay, for a certain purpose or group

MAIN IDEAS

Read the sentences. Then number them in the order that the ideas appear in Reading 2.

_____ a. PSAs provide people with information about things like medical problems.

_____ b. Professional sports depend on advertising.

_____ c. Advertising helps support the arts.

_____ d. Ads provide us with helpful information about products we want to buy.

_____ e. Advertisements make the world more colorful.

_____ f. Ads help pay for the services that websites provide.

DETAILS

Write an example for each of the benefits of advertising listed in the chart.

Benefit	Example
provides information for buying something	_best deal for new car in newspaper_
supports the arts	
helps support sports	
public service announcements inform the public	
helps make the world more colorful	

 WHAT DO YOU THINK?

A. Discuss the questions in a group.

1. Some people say that advertising is a "necessary evil." What does this mean? Do you agree? Why or why not? (If something is _evil,_ it is very bad.)

2. Would you be willing to pay more for things and have no advertising?

B. Think about both Reading 1 and Reading 2 as you discuss the questions. Then choose one question and write five to eight sentences in response.

1. Think of an advertisement that you've seen recently that affected you. What was it selling? How did it affect you? Was it positive or negative?

2. Do you think there is too much advertising? Where would you like to see less or no advertising?

A **suffix** is a group of letters that comes at the end of a word, such as *-ful* in *painful*. When you add a suffix to a word, it changes the part of speech. Being familiar with suffixes can help you increase your vocabulary. Here is a list of suffixes.

Adjective	Noun	Adverb
-ful	-ment	-ly
-able	-tion	
-ial	-ship	
-er	-ness	

Tip for Success

Being familiar with suffixes used to form nouns and adjectives will help you in your writing and in your reading comprehension.

Read the words. Decide which part of speech they are based on their suffixes. Then check (✓) the correct column.

	Adjective	Noun	Adverb
1. unpredictable	____	____	____
2. relationship	____	____	____
3. recently	____	____	____
4. painful	____	____	____
5. dissatisfaction	____	____	____
6. distrustful	____	____	____
7. happiness	____	____	____
8. donation	____	____	____
9. certainly	____	____	____
10. colorful	____	____	____

WRITING

A Letter to the Editor

In Unit 3, you learned about writing an opinion paragraph. You can use this type of writing in a longer form, such as in a **letter to the editor**. A letter to the editor is sent to the editor of a newspaper or magazine and expresses the writer's opinion about an issue. These letters are often published.

In longer pieces of writing, each paragraph has a purpose. In a letter to the editor, the first paragraph is the **introductory paragraph**. It describes a situation and gives your opinion of it. The next paragraphs are the **body paragraphs**, which give specific reasons for your opinion and examples to make it a strong argument. Finally, the **concluding paragraph** is the last paragraph. It restates your opinion, summarizes your reasons for it, and often gives a prediction about it.

A. Read the letter to the editor of a newspaper.

Dear Editor,

Introductory paragraph

Recently, I was watching TV with my young son, age 13, when he pointed out to me, "Oh, look. The detective uses an Apple computer." How did he know that? I asked myself, but then I recognized the familiar logo. I started watching the show more carefully and saw four more products appear on the screen before the show ended. I found out that this is something called *product placement*. Through product placement, advertisers pay to have their products appear not only in TV shows, but also in movies and music videos. We are watching commercials without our knowledge. I think product placement is horrible and should be banned from television.

Body paragraph

First of all, there is already too much advertising in our lives, and we don't need any more. We are all constantly faced with advertisements. You can't drive down a major road without seeing huge billboards advertising products from fast food to phone services. Buses, subways, trains, and even taxicabs are covered with advertisements. Before watching a movie now, you have to sit through ten minutes of commercials. I read a report in the newspaper that said you could see as many as 50 products in the broadcast of one TV show. And if you watch cable TV, that number jumps to almost 1,000 products per show!

Body paragraph — But a second, more important reason that product placement should be banned is that it's done without my permission. In a sense, I feel that my freedom is being taken away from me. When a traditional TV commercial comes on, I can choose to watch it or not, and I'm aware that products are being advertised. However, product placement just appears in the middle of a show that I'm watching for entertainment. I can't turn off or tune out the advertising part without turning off the entertainment. I'm forced to watch various brand names and logos appear in the middle of my favorite show, and I can't do anything about it.

Concluding paragraph — I think there is far too much advertising. If I want to relax by watching television, I should not have to be exposed to advertising in the middle of my program. Additionally, I feel that I have the right to know when I'm watching a commercial. That's why I think product placement should be banned from television before everything on television becomes one very long commercial.

Sincerely,

A Concerned Citizen

Tip for Success

Remember to always include a greeting, such as *Dear Editor*, and a polite ending using a word like *Sincerely* in all of your formal letters.

B. Reread the letter to the editor in Activity A. Then answer the questions.

1. What is the writer's opinion? Underline the sentence, or part of the sentence that gives the opinion.

2. What are the first reason and example that the writer gives for his or her opinion?

   Reason: _____

   Example: _____

3. What are the second reason and example that the writer gives for his or her opinion?

   Reason: _____

   Example: _____

4. Underline the concluding sentence. Write the part of the concluding sentence that gives a prediction.

   _____

A **simple sentence** contains a *subject* and a *verb* and expresses a complete thought or idea. A simple sentence is sometimes called an *independent clause*.

> Usha drives to work every day.
> $\underset{\text{subject}}{\underline{\text{Usha}}}$ $\underset{\text{verb}}{\underline{\text{drives}}}$ to work every day.

A **compound sentence** contains two **independent clauses** (or simple sentences) joined by a **coordinating conjunction**, such as *and*, *but*, *so*, and *or*. A comma usually comes before the coordinating conjunction in a compound sentence.

Use *and* to combine two sentences with related ideas.

> The ad was very funny, **and** it gave us helpful information.

Use *but* to combine two sentences with contrasting ideas.

> We enjoyed the movie, **but** it had a very sad ending.

Use *so* when the second sentence is a result of the first sentence.

> Ali isn't feeling well, **so** he isn't coming to class today.

Use *or* when there is a choice or two possibilities.

> You can take the train to Madrid, **or** you can fly.

Using different types of sentences can help make your writing more interesting for your reader.

A. Complete each sentence with *and*, *or*, *but*, or *so*. Then write the reason you chose that conjunction (*related ideas*, *contrasting ideas*, *a result*, or *a choice*).

1. I am the mother of young children, __and__ I feel that all advertising during children's programming should be banned.

    reason: _____ related ideas _____

2. The movie was about a very serious topic, _____ there were some very funny moments in it.

    reason: _____

3. Children are exposed to many advertisements for unhealthy foods, _____ parents have to educate their children about good food and nutrition.

    reason: _____

4. Many people love to watch sports on television, _____ it's a lot more exciting seeing sports at a stadium.

   reason:_____

5. We can discuss the report today, _____ we can wait until tomorrow.

   reason:_____

B. Combine the sentences with *and*, *or*, *but*, or *so*. Add commas.

1. I like to stay healthy. I exercise every day.

   _____

2. Sara Marcone is a very creative writer. She has written five novels.

   _____

3. The concert was entertaining. It was a bit too long.

   _____

4. We receive a lot of mail that advertises sales. Not everything in the store is on sale.

   _____

5. She writes a humorous column in the newspaper. I enjoy reading it every week.

   _____

6. We can go out for dinner. We can stay home.

   _____

C. Write five compound sentences in your notebook. Use each conjunction (*and*, *or*, *but*, and *so*) at least once.

Unit Assignment   **Write a letter to the editor**

 In this assignment, you are going to write a four-paragraph letter to the editor. As you prepare your letter, think about the Unit Question, "Does advertising help or harm us?" Be sure to give your opinion with at least two reasons. Refer to the Self-Assessment checklist on page 130. Use information from Readings 1 and 2 and your work in this unit to support your ideas.

For alternative unit assignments, see the *Q: Skills for Success Teacher's Handbook*.

PLAN AND WRITE

A. BRAINSTORM Think about your answer to the Unit Question, "Does advertising help or harm us?" Then write a list of reasons and examples for your answer or opinion in your notebook.

B. PLAN Follow these steps to plan your letter to the editor.

1. Read your list from Activity A. Circle your best reasons and examples.

2. Write an outline for your letter.

   A. **Introductory paragraph:** Write a topic sentence to give your opinion.

   _____

   _____

   Explain how you formed your opinion.

   _____

   _____

   B. **Body paragraph 1:** Explain one of the reasons for your opinion with a specific example.

   _____

   _____

   _____

   _____

   C. **Body paragraph 2:** Explain a second reason for your opinion with a specific example.

   _____

   _____

   _____

   _____

D. **Concluding paragraph:** Write a concluding sentence that restates your opinion.

_____

_____

Summarize the reasons for your opinion.

_____

_____

C. **WRITE** Write your letter to the editor in your notebook. Use your outline from Activity B. Remember to state your opinion in your introductory paragraph and include two body paragraphs. Look at the Self-Assessment checklist below to guide your writing.

REVISE AND EDIT

 **Your Writing Process**

For this activity, you could also use Stage 2A, *Self Review* in *Q Online Practice*.

A. **PEER REVIEW** Read a partner's letter. Answer the questions and discuss them with your partner.

1. Is there a clear opinion on whether advertising helps or harms us in the introductory paragraph? Underline it.

2. Are there two body paragraphs with reasons for the opinion?

3. Is a specific example given for each reason?

4. Does the concluding paragraph restate the opinion? Underline it.

B. **REWRITE** Review the answers to the questions in Activity A. You may want to revise and rewrite your letter to the editor.

C. **EDIT** Complete the Self-Assessment checklist as you prepare to write the final draft of your letter to the editor. Be prepared to hand in your work or discuss it in class.

SELF-ASSESSMENT		
Yes	**No**	
☐	☐	Is the punctuation correct?
☐	☐	If words with suffixes are used, are they correct?
☐	☐	Does the letter include vocabulary from the unit?
☐	☐	Does the letter include an introductory paragraph, two body paragraphs, and a concluding paragraph?
☐	☐	Does the writer use some compound sentences with *and, or, but,* or *so* to vary the length of sentences?

Circle the words you learned in this unit.

Nouns
broadcasting
consequence 🔑 AWL
dissatisfaction
donation
exposure AWL
happiness 🔑
possession 🔑
relationship 🔑

Verbs
entertain 🔑
imply 🔑 AWL
support 🔑

Adjectives
annoying 🔑
annual 🔑 AWL
colorful
distrustful
memorable
painful 🔑
recent 🔑
surrounding 🔑
trivial
unpredictable AWL

Adverbs
certainly 🔑
recently 🔑

Phrasal Verb
tune out

Idiom
means to an end

🔑 Oxford 3000™ words
AWL Academic Word List

Check (✓) the skills you learned. If you need more work on a skill, refer to the page(s) in parentheses.

READING	⚪	I can distinguish facts from opinions. (p. 119)
VOCABULARY	⚪	I can use suffixes. (p. 124)
WRITING	⚪	I can write a letter to the editor. (p. 125)
GRAMMAR	⚪	I can use compound sentences. (p. 127)
LEARNING OUTCOME	⚫	I can write a multiple-paragraph letter to the editor expressing my opinion about advertising.

Unit QUESTION

Why do people take risks?

PREVIEW THE UNIT

A Discuss these questions with your classmates.

What does "take a risk" mean?

Are you a risk-taker? If so, what kind of risks?

Look at the photo. Why is the person taking this risk?

B Discuss the Unit Question above with your classmates.

Listen to *The Q Classroom*, Track 8 on CD 2, to hear other answers.

C Look at the photos. Number them in order of risk. Use 1 for the riskiest and 6 for the least risky. Then compare your answers with a partner and discuss why you made your choices.

____ skiing

____ mountain climbing

____ rock climbing

____ motocross

____ white-water rafting

____ bungee jumping

D Look at the photos. Which job do you think is the most dangerous? Number them from 1 to 6. Use 1 for the most dangerous. Then compare your answers with your partner and discuss why you made your choices.

____ steelworker

____ logger

____ roofer

____ farmer

____ fisherman

____ painter

| **Fear Factor: Success and Risk in Extreme Sports**

VOCABULARY

Here are some words from Reading 1. Read the sentences. Circle the answer that best matches the meaning of each bold word.

1. Running a marathon requires both physical strength and strong **mental** qualities like confidence and determination.
    a. relating to the mind
    b. relating to the body

2. During the summer months, some of her athletic **pursuits** are running, biking, and mountain climbing.
    a. activities
    b. teammates

3. In order to really enjoy skiing, you need to have a very high **tolerance** for the cold.
    a. ability to accept something difficult or unpleasant
    b. knowledge about a subject

4. Joe Simpson is **notable** for his mountain climbing as well as his writing.
    a. intelligent
    b. important and well-known

5. He's an experienced climber, and now he believes he's ready for the **challenge** of climbing Mount Everest.
    a. something fun and relaxing
    b. something difficult and exciting

6. My memory of reaching the top of the mountain is so **vivid** that I feel as if I'm still there.
    a. causing pain or discomfort
    b. producing a strong, clear picture in your mind

7. People **perceive** farming as a safe job, but it is one of the riskiest jobs a person can have.
    a. think of
    b. recognize the importance of

8. If you go rock climbing, you should take **precautions**, such as wearing a helmet and the right kind of shoes.

   a. things you do to avoid danger

   b. things you do well

9. One **aspect** of extreme sports that many people cannot overcome is the risk.

   a. part

   b. result

10. One **trait** that extreme sports athletes share is the love of excitement in their sport.

    a. particular quality

    b. problem

PREVIEW READING 1

You are going to read an article from *National Geographic News* that looks at why some people do extreme sports. Extreme sports are sports that most people think are very risky.

Read the first sentence of each paragaph. Why do you think people do things like extreme sports? Check (✓) your ideas.

☐ They don't think it's too risky.

☐ They secretly want to get hurt.

☐ They like a challenge.

☐ They love the feeling of excitement.

☐ It makes them focus on the present moment.

☐ They want to be famous.

☐ Other reasons _____

_____

Read the article.

Fear Factor: Success and Risk in Extreme Sports

1 Every year in Pamplona, Spain, hundreds of people run alongside 1,300-pound (600-kilo) bulls, just for the fun of it. And every year at least a few of these people are injured, some seriously. Yet this does not stop people from participating in the event.

2 What is it that drives some people to embrace extreme risks, while the rest of us run to the safety of the sidelines[1]? Lester Keller, a longtime coach and sports-psychology coordinator for the U.S. Ski and Snowboard Association, says that not everyone has the **mental** character to excel in dangerous **pursuits**. He notes that most of us reach a point that limits our appetite for extreme risk and, as a result, our ability to perform well in dangerous conditions. But others have a much higher **tolerance** for risk. Take the example of Daron Rahlves, a top U.S. downhill ski racer. "The high element of risk makes you feel alive, tests what you are made of and how far you can take yourself," Rahlves said in a previous interview with U.S. Ski Team staff. "I'm not looking for danger. I'm in it for the **challenge**, my heart thumping as I finish, the feeling of being alive," he said. "I definitely get scared on some of the courses. It just makes me fight more... That's when I do best."

3 The fear that drives many people away from the risks of extreme sports may be the same ingredient that keeps others coming back for more. Mountaineer Al Read has logged many **notable** first ascents[2] over the course of his climbing career. Having climbed for over 40 years, Read says he no longer pushes to the extremes as he once did— but the feeling is still **vivid**. "I can remember when I was getting into situations where I thought that at any moment I could be killed," he told *National Geographic News*. "... I would say, '... I'll never do this again.' But we'd get back down, and when we were safe we'd say, 'Man was that great!'" he recalled. "You forget how scary it was, and you go back again."

4 In addition to not being afraid of risks, certain people may **perceive** risk differently from others. Shane Murphy, a sports psychologist and professor at Western Connecticut State University, has worked with Olympians and other athletes. He says he is struck by the way they redefine risk according to their skills, experience, and environment. He worked with a group climbing Everest without oxygen, which to him was the riskiest thing anyone could do. But the climbers took every **precaution** to prepare themselves for this climb. As Murphy describes it, "To them it was the next step in an activity that they've done for

---

[1] **sidelines:** the lines that form the edges of a sports field   [2] **ascent:** a climb to the top of a mountain

years. They weren't going out there to get hurt." Murphy said the perspective of extreme athletes is very different from our own. "We look at a risky situation and know that if we were in that situation, we would be out of control," he said. "But from the athletes' perspective, they have a lot of control, and there are a lot of things that they do to minimize risk." Statistically, mountain climbing is not as risky as people think it is. Our perceived risk of the sport leaves the majority of us at the bottom of the mountain.

5   Another key **aspect** of risk perception may be something referred to as "the flow" or "the zone." It is a state in which many athletes describe becoming absorbed in pursuits that focus the mind completely on the present. "Something that makes you begin climbing, perhaps, is that your adrenaline flows and you become very concentrated on what you're doing," Read said. "After it's over there's exhilaration[3]. You wouldn't have that same feeling if the risk hadn't been there." Psychologists note that some people seem to have a strong craving for adrenaline rushes[4] as a thrill-seeking behavior or personality **trait**. As a result, these types of people may always be driven to adventures that others consider extreme. "I can enjoy hitting the tennis ball around, because that's my skill level," Murphy said. "But others might need the challenge of Olympic competition."

[3] **exhilaration:** a feeling of being very happy and alive
[4] **adrenaline rush:** a feeling of being very excited and happy, brought about from the body chemical of the same name

Main Ideas

Write the correct paragraph number next to each main idea.

____ 1. Some people may have a stronger desire than others for risks because of the adrenaline flow that they get.

____ 2. Certain people may perceive risk differently from the rest of us.

____ 3. People who enjoy the risks of extreme sports also enjoy the fear.

____ 4. Not everyone has the same tolerance for risk; some of us have a much higher tolerance.

DETAILS

Complete each statement with information from Reading 1.

1. Every year in Pamplona, Spain, hundreds of people run alongside bulls, just for _____.

2. Lester Keller says that not everyone has the _____ to excel in dangerous pursuits.

3. Al Read remembers getting into situations where he thought that at any moment he _____.

4. Shane Murphy worked with a group climbing Mount Everest _____.

5. Statistically, mountain climbing is not as risky as _____.

 WHAT DO YOU THINK?

Discuss the questions in a group. Then choose one question and write five to eight sentences in response.

1. Think of an activity that you perceive to be risky. Why do you think it is risky? Give specific reasons. How would someone who does this activity frequently feel differently about it from someone who doesn't? Why?

2. Look back at the photos of the jobs on page 134. According to the latest statistics (the number of deaths per 100,000), the most dangerous job pictured is a fisherman. Did you rate fishing as a very dangerous job? Why or why not?

3. Why do you think we perceive activities such as mountain climbing to be riskier than they actually are?

A **referent** is a word or group of words that refers to a noun that was mentioned previously. Understanding referents will help you become a better reader. In Reading 1, the writer is focusing on what makes one group of people (those who enjoy extreme sports) different from everyone else (those who do not enjoy extreme sports). The writer uses certain words and phrases to refer to each group throughout the reading.

Group 1 (The Minority)	Group 2 (The Majority)
People who enjoy extreme sports	**People who don't enjoy extreme sports**
some people	the rest of us
others	most of us
certain people	many people
they	we
these types of people	

referent: people who don't enjoy extreme sports

He notes that <u>most of us</u> reach a point that limits our appetite for extreme risk …

referent: people who enjoy extreme sports

But <u>others</u> have a much higher tolerance for risk.

A. Read the sentences from Reading 1. Underline words that refer to people who enjoy extreme sports. Circle words that refer to the majority of people.

1. What is it that drives some people to embrace extreme risks, while the rest of us run to the safety of the sidelines?

2. He notes that most of us reach a point that limits our appetite for extreme risk … But others have a much higher tolerance for risk.

3. The fear that drives many people away from the risks of extreme sports may be the same ingredient that keeps others coming back for more.

4. In addition to not being afraid of risks, certain people may perceive risk differently from others.

5. As a result, these types of people may always be driven to adventures that others consider extreme.

B. Read the paragraph about the types of people who choose to become fishermen. Underline the words and phrases that refer to the fishermen. Circle the words and phrases that refer to the majority of people.

The Life of a Fisherman

What does it take to become a fisherman? It's definitely not for most of us. The majority of people will not want to earn their living on the dangerous seas, working 24 hours, seven days a week, until enough fish are caught. However, some people enjoy the challenge of this type of work. These types of people would not be happy sitting at a desk from nine to five. For them, making a lot of money in a short amount of time is worth the risk. The rest of us would probably prefer our boring lifestyles without the risk. It takes a certain type of person who is willing to be on a boat for three to five months in order to make a living. Perhaps it's the thrill of the unknown that certain types of people look for. The rest of us are content to watch the boats from the safety of the harbor.

READING 2 | The Climb of My Life

VOCABULARY

Here are some words from Reading 2. Read their definitions. Then complete each sentence.

bravely (*adv.*) showing readiness to do dangerous or difficult things without showing fear

conquer (*v.*) to overcome something

determined (*adj.*) firmly decided to succeed in doing something, even if it is difficult

distinctive (*adj.*) clearly different from others and therefore easy to recognize

earn (*v.*) to get something that you deserve

goal (*n.*) a purpose or aim

role (*n.*) a person's part in something such as a play, movie, or life

significant (*adj.*) important or large enough to be noticed

ultimate (*adj.*) the greatest, best, or worst

1. My _____ for this year is to train until I am ready to run the city marathon.

2. My husband took a class that helped him _____ his fear of flying. Now he can ride in airplanes without feeling so nervous.

3. We were very tired, but we didn't give up. We were _____ to get to the top of the mountain.

4. The firefighters _____ entered the burning school to rescue the children.

5. When our parents were away, my oldest sister took on the _____ of the family guardian.

6. I always recognize Dina on the phone because she has a very _____ voice. She doesn't sound like any of my other friends.

7. When we were children, we had to do work around the house in order to _____ rewards like toys or candy.

8. Rock climbing is the _____ activity for people who want a fun, exciting challenge.

9. Volunteering in South America was one of the most _____ experiences of my life. It inspired me to pursue a career in public service.

PREVIEW READING 2

You are going to read an excerpt from a book called *The Climb of My Life: Scaling Mountains with a Borrowed Heart* by Kelly Perkins. It's about a woman who climbs a mountain ten months after having a heart transplant. A transplant is a type of surgery in which an organ, for example, a heart, liver, or kidney, is replaced.

Read the title and the first two paragraphs. Why do you think Kelly took this risk? Write your ideas.

_____

_____

Read the excerpt from the book.

The Climb of My Life

1   *At the age of 30, Kelly Perkins developed a disease of the heart, and after three years of treatment, she received a heart transplant. Ten months later, she climbed to the top of Half Dome, a mountain in Yosemite National Park in the United States, and became the first heart transplant patient to do so.*

2   Like life, mountains can be seen as a series of difficulties that you need to overcome. To me, a mountain is the **ultimate** challenge, with body, spirit, and mind all having to work together. Being sick is a challenge, too. Both challenges involve **bravely** facing the unknown, and to **conquer** either requires well-defined **goals** and discipline. Of the two, of course, I'd rather the mountain be my physical challenge than physical challenges be my "mountain."

3   Mountains began to consume my thoughts. Secretly, I wanted to do something **significant** to help change the image that friends and family had developed of me. I had been cast in the **role** of patient. In spite of being very good in that role, I hated being a patient and desperately wanted to change my image. I wanted bruises to be **earned** from sports-related activities, not from needle pricks and aspirin-thinned blood. At this stage, my self-image was as important to my well-being as anything else. If, I figured, I could rebuild my strength and regain at least some of my former athleticism, an improved image would naturally follow.

4   I set a goal—to hike the 4,100-foot ascent of Half Dome in Yosemite. I was drawn to this destination by its beauty, a beauty not because it was perfect, but because it was imperfect. Half Dome's shape is unforgettably **distinctive** because it's broken. If it were whole, it would lose its uniqueness. The spirit-building message wasn't lost on me. Just because I wasn't perfect didn't mean I couldn't stand as tall and mighty as anyone else.

5   In August of 1996, just ten months after my heart replacement, my husband Craig and I began to hike the trail leading to Half Dome. The trail began with a mild incline, which we eagerly took at a brisk pace. I was winded at first, but as soon as my heart caught up with me, I felt energized. I tried to go as fast as the other hikers, but found it difficult to keep up. The canyon had many steep slopes and deep stone stairs, allowing in very little sunlight, which kept temperatures cool and the rocks slippery.

6   Though the climb's final half-mile isn't technically difficult, the granite dome, angled at 45 degrees, can be extremely intimidating, especially for those afraid of heights. The last 500 feet to the summit looks like the "stairway to heaven."

There was a handrail made out of steel cables, connected to stairs made of thin wooden planks. Thrown along the stairs were weathered work gloves, available to help protect the climbers' hands from the "death grip" commonly used during descent. Craig, observing the daunting task ahead, gently asked, "Are you sure you want to continue?" **Determined** to reap[1] the reward for all my effort, I replied, "Absolutely, we have to go on." Step for step, Craig stayed directly behind me, providing a welcome sense of security. When I finally reached the top, I was overcome with joy. Ten months after my transplant, I had reached the top of Half Dome! My new heart had not failed me.

7   Craig and I made our way over to the edge. Pausing to peer into the valley below, we stood in silence, amazed at how far we had come. As if the moment itself was not enough, Craig surprised me with a gold charm[2] in the shape of Half Dome. He said, "This is the first mountain to add to the bracelet I gave you …" As I held the handcrafted ornament in my hand, I was amazed at its likeness. It was smooth on the back, resembling the perfectly bell-shaped dome, the front being chiseled, replicating its famous broken granite face. Craig took a moment to express how proud he was of me, saying, "When you were really sick and I had to carry you up the stairs at night, I always looked at the famous Ansel Adams photo of Half Dome hung on the stairway wall and wondered if we'd ever make another climb." His tender words brought me to tears. We had done it; we were here at the top of the mountain—a long way from those nights of not knowing what the future would bring.

[1] **reap:** to receive a benefit due to one's efforts
[2] **charm:** a small piece of jewelry often worn on bracelets

Main Ideas

Read the sentences. Then number them in the order that they happened.

_____ a. Kelly decided to climb Half Dome Mountain in Yosemite.

_____ b. Ten months after her heart replacement, Kelly began to climb Half Dome.

_____ c. Kelly decided that she wanted to climb a mountain to change her image.

_____ d. Kelly became very sick and received a heart transplant.

_____ e. Craig was very proud of Kelly's accomplishment.

_____ f. Kelly reached the top of Half Dome with a new heart.

Details

Complete each statement with information from Reading 2.

1. Kelly chose a mountain to climb that is _____ feet high.

2. One reason she chose this mountain is because, like her, it is

    _____.

3. Kelly began her climb of Half Dome with her husband in August of

    _____.

4. The last half-mile of the climb is hard if you're afraid of heights because it's angled at _____ degrees.

5. There is a rough stairway to help climbers for the last

    _____ feet.

6. Kelly's husband Craig said it was the first mountain to add to

    _____ that he gave her.

WHAT DO YOU THINK?

A. Discuss the questions in a group.

1. In Paragraph 1, Kelly talks about challenges—climbing mountains and being sick—and says, "Of the two, of course, I'd rather the mountain be my physical challenge than physical challenges be my 'mountain.'" What does this mean for Kelly?

2. Kelly Perkins climbed mountains before and after her heart transplant. Do you think the reasons for climbing mountains were different before and after her transplant? Why or why not?

B. Think about both Reading 1 and Reading 2 as you discuss the questions. Then choose one question and write five to eight sentences in response.

1. Do you think that people who do extreme sports would not be happy if they didn't continue to take risks? In other words, do you think they need to take risks?

2. Do you think people can change the way they perceive risk? Are there certain situations or times in people's lives when we perceive activities as being more or less risky?

| Vocabulary Skill | Using the dictionary | |

Finding the correct meaning

Words often have more than one meaning. When dictionaries include more than one meaning, the different definitions are usually numbered. When you are using a dictionary to find the correct meaning for a word, it is important to read the entire sentence and consider the context.

Look at the example and the dictionary definitions that follow it. Definition number four is correct.

> **Example:** Mountains began to **consume** my thoughts.

> **con·sume** **AWL** /kən'sum/ *verb* [T] (*written*) **1** to use something such as fuel, energy, or time: *25 percent of the world's population consumes 80 percent of the planet's resources.* **2** to eat or drink something: *to consume calories* **3** (used about fire) to destroy something **4** (used about an emotion) to affect someone very strongly: *She was consumed by grief when her son was killed.*

All dictionary entries are from the *Oxford American Dictionary for learners of English* © Oxford University Press 2011.

A. Read the sentences from Reading 1 and Reading 2. Look up the underlined words in your dictionary and write the correct definition based on the context. Then compare your answers with a partner.

Reading 1:

1. What is it that <u>drives</u> some people to <u>embrace</u> extreme risks, while the rest of us run to the safety of the sidelines?

    drive: _____

    embrace: _____

2. He notes that most of us reach a point that limits our <u>appetite</u> for extreme risk ...

    appetite: _____

3. The fear that drives many people away from the risks of extreme sports may be the same <u>ingredient</u> that keeps others coming back for more.

    ingredient: _____

Reading 2:

4. I had been cast in the <u>role</u> of patient.

    role: _____

5. I wanted bruises to be <u>earned</u> from sports-related activities, not from needle pricks and aspirin-thinned blood.

    earned: _____

6. It was smooth on the back, resembling the perfectly bell-shaped dome, the front being chiseled, replicating its famous broken granite <u>face</u>.

    face: _____

B. Choose three words from Activity A. Write a sentence using each word.

1. _____

    _____

2. _____

    _____

3. _____

    _____

WRITING

| Writing Skill | Writing a narrative essay | |

An essay is a piece of writing that has more than two paragraphs. A **narrative essay** describes a personal experience and includes three important parts: an **introductory paragraph**, the *body paragraphs*, and a *concluding statement*.

The introductory paragraph gives necessary background information and gives the main idea of the essay. In a narrative essay, the introductory paragraph describes why this is an important or memorable story for the writer and perhaps what the writer learned from this experience.

The body of a narrative essay includes one to three paragraphs that describe the events, including interesting details such as facts, examples, or explanations to support the main idea of the essay. The concluding statement of a narrative essay restates the main idea and summarizes why this story is an important one for the writer.

A. Read the narrative essay.

The Second Climb

A few months after the Half Dome climb, I decided to climb Mt. Whitney in California. I had always wanted to climb Mount Whitney. There were several reasons for choosing this mountain as my next conquest. First of all, it is the tallest mountain in the continental United States. Second, when I looked back at my climb to the top of it eleven years earlier, I considered it my greatest pre-transplant hiking accomplishment.

Many healthy people hike Whitney in two days. Some even manage to go up and down the same day. We took three days. We wanted to make it to the summit and back safely. On the third day of our trip … at 2:30 p.m., we all gathered under a spectacular blue sky to walk the final steps to the geographical marker identifying the summit, the highest point on the continental United States.

Tears rolled down our faces. Everyone knew how much this accomplishment meant to me. I had made it to the peak, this time with a second heart and my husband. I truly felt on top of the world. I raised my hands in victory and cried out to Craig, "We did it!"

B. Reread the narrative essay in Activity A. Then answer the questions.

1. Where does the writer give background information? Put a check mark (✓) next to it.

2. Which sentence in the introductory paragraph includes the main idea of the narrative? Write it below.

_____

3. How many body paragraphs does the writer include? Mark the body paragraph(s) with brackets. ([ ])

4. What details does the writer include that help make the narrative interesting? Underline them.

5. Which sentence in the concluding paragraph explains why this story is important to the writer? Write it below.

_____

Grammar | Shifts between past and present

A written essay or passage begins with a specific time frame, such as past, present, or future. Sometimes writers use one time frame for the entire passage, but often they shift or change time frames. Writers shift time frames according to what they are describing.

Writers often use the **simple past** to begin a story, or set the scene.

> simple past
> A few months after the Half Dome climb, I **decided** to climb Mt. Whitney in California.

Writers use the **past perfect** to describe things that happened before the events in the story. Use **had + past participle** to form the past perfect.

> simple past
> Secretly, I **wanted** to do something significant to help change the image that
> past perfect
> friends and family **had developed** of me.

Writers use the **simple present** to describe things or give certain facts or information.

> simple present   simple present
> Half Dome's shape **is** unforgettably distinctive because it**'s** broken.

A. Look back at the narrative essay on page 148. Underline the simple past verbs and the past perfect verbs. Circle the simple present verbs. Then compare your answers with a partner.

B. Read the short passages. Write *present/present* if the passage uses only a present time frame. Write *past* if the passage uses only a past time frame. Write *present/past* or *past/present* if the passage changes time frames.

1. ___past / present___ Three years ago, I went hiking in the White Mountains in New Hampshire. New Hampshire is a beautiful place to hike with lots of lakes and mountains.

2. _____ The storm last week caused a lot of damage, and many people could not get to work or school. Now the roads are clear, and businesses and schools are open again.

3. _____ Florence, Italy is a wonderful place to spend a vacation. There are lots of interesting things to do and see, and the food is delicious.

4. _____ Last year, Amy decided to try rock climbing. It was something she had never done, but had always wanted to try.

5. _____ Mountain climbing is exciting, but it can be very dangerous. Last year, there were hundreds of mountain-climbing accidents. Many of the climbers were very experienced.

C. Complete each sentence using a different time frame.

1. I used to drive to work, but now _____I ride my bike_____.

2. I used to drink soda every day. Then my dentist told me it was bad

   for my teeth. Now _____.

3. When I was younger, I didn't speak English very well.

   Now _____.

4. Many things are different in my country now. For example, in the

   past, _____.

5. I used to eat every meal in a restaurant. I'm trying to save money,

   so now _____.

6. I used to watch TV all weekend, but now _____

   _____.

In this assignment, you are going to write a narrative essay in which you describe a time when you took a risk. As you prepare your essay, think about the Unit Question, "Why do people take risks?" Refer to the Self-Assessment checklist on page 152. Use information from Readings 1 and 2 and your work in this unit to support your ideas.

For alternative unit assignments, see the Q: Skills for Success Teacher's Handbook.

Tip) Critical Thinking

In the unit assignment, you will write a narrative essay, **reporting** on a specific time and series of events. When you report something, whether it is a description of an event or the results of a study, you pull from a wide variety of facts and details to create a coherent story or narrative. This allows you to use information in the way that is most helpful to you.

PLAN AND WRITE

A. BRAINSTORM Think of some risks that you've taken. They can be small or big risks. Write as many as you can in your notebook.

B. PLAN Choose one of the risks that you wrote down in Activity A. Then write an outline of your ideas.

1. **Introductory paragraph:** Write the risk you took.

   _____

   _____

   Provide some background information.

   _____

   _____

   Write a sentence explaining why this risk was important to you.

   _____

   _____

2. **Body paragraph 1:** Briefly write the events of the story. Include details.

   _____

   _____

   _____

3. **Body paragraph 2:** Continue with the events of the story. Include details.

   _____

   _____

   _____

4. **Concluding statement:** Briefly restate the risk you took and summarize why this was important for you.

_____

_____

C. **WRITE** Write your essay in your notebook. Use your outline from Activity B. Describe the events that took place in two body paragraphs. In your concluding paragraph, be sure to restate the risk and summarize why it was important to you. Look at the Self-Assessment checklist below to guide your writing.

REVISE AND EDIT

A. **PEER REVIEW** Read a partner's essay. Answer the questions and discuss them with your partner.

1. Is the risk described clearly in the introductory paragraph?

2. Are the events of the story described in two body paragraphs?

3. Does the concluding statement restate the risk that was taken and summarize why it was important?

B. **REWRITE** Review the answers to the questions in Activity A. You may want to revise and rewrite your essay.

C. **EDIT** Complete the Self-Assessment checklist as you prepare to write the final draft of your narrative essay. Be prepared to hand in your work or discuss it in class.

SELF-ASSESSMENT		
Yes	**No**	
☐	☐	Is the punctuation correct?
☐	☐	Are all words used in their correct forms?
☐	☐	Are all words spelled correctly?
☐	☐	Does the essay include vocabulary from the unit?
☐	☐	Does the essay begin with an introductory paragraph that gives the reason the person took the risk and any important background information?
☐	☐	Does the essay include two body paragraphs that include events and details?
☐	☐	Does the essay include a concluding statement that restates the risk and summarizes why it is important to the writer?
☐	☐	Does the essay shift between present and past correctly?

Circle the words you learned in this unit.

Nouns
appetite
aspect AWL 🔑
challenge AWL 🔑
face 🔑
goal AWL 🔑
ingredient 🔑
precaution
pursuit AWL
role AWL 🔑

tolerance
trait

Verbs
conquer
consume AWL
drive 🔑
earn 🔑
embrace
perceive AWL

Adjectives
determined 🔑
distinctive AWL
mental 🔑 AWL
notable
significant AWL 🔑
ultimate AWL 🔑
vivid

Adverb
bravely

🔑 Oxford 3000™ words
AWL Academic Word List

Check (✓) the skills you learned. If you need more work on a skill, refer to the page(s) in parentheses.

READING	●	I can use referents to understand contrast. (p. 140)
VOCABULARY	●	I can use the dictionary to find correct meanings. (p. 146)
WRITING	●	I can write a narrative essay. (p. 148)
GRAMMAR	●	I can use time shifts correctly in narrative writing. (p. 149)
LEARNING OUTCOME	●	I can develop a narrative essay describing a risk I have taken.

UNIT 8

Cities/Urban Lives

READING ●	making inferences
VOCABULARY ●	participles as adjectives
WRITING ●	writing a problem/solution essay; thesis statements
GRAMMAR ●	passive voice

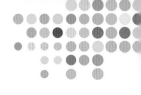

Q ?

Unit QUESTION

How can we make cities better places to live?

PREVIEW THE UNIT

A **Discuss these questions with your classmates.**

Do you like where you live? Why or why not?

Many people are starting to believe that "green" (environmentally friendly) cities are desirable places to live. Do you agree? Why or why not?

Look at the photo. What is the woman doing? Why?

B **Discuss the Unit Question above with your classmates.**

Listen to *The Q Classroom*, Track 11 on CD 2, to hear other answers.

C Take the quiz to find out about your carbon footprint. Circle your answers.

Carbon Footprint Quiz

A "carbon footprint" refers to the total amount of gasses released into the environment from an individual, group of people, activity, or product. Take this quiz to find out about your personal carbon footprint.

1. **How do you usually travel to work or school?**
   a. I walk or ride my bicycle.
   b. I take public transportation (subway, bus, train, etc.).
   c. I drive.

2. **How often do you eat meat?**
   a. never
   b. sometimes
   c. frequently, with most meals

3. **What kind of bags do you use when you buy groceries?**
   a. reusable cloth bags
   b. paper bags
   c. plastic bags

4. **Where do you live?**
   a. in a large apartment building
   b. in a small apartment building
   c. in a house

5. **How much paper do you use?**
   a. Not much because I mostly read online.
   b. Some. I read online, but often print out emails, articles, etc.
   c. A lot. Reading online hurts my eyes, so I print out lots of emails, articles, etc.

PUT AN END TO PLASTIC BAGS

How big is your carbon footprint? Find out below.

- If you answered mostly *a*, you have a fairly small carbon footprint. Keep up the good work!
- If you answered mostly *b*, you're doing OK, but there are things you can do to reduce your carbon footprint.
- If you answered mostly *c*, you probably have a large carbon footprint. You should think about ways you can become "greener."

D Discuss the results of the quiz with a partner. What are some things you can do to reduce your carbon footprint?

READING

READING 1 | New Zero-Carbon City to Be Built

VOCABULARY

Here are some words from Reading 1. Read their definitions. Then complete the email message.

---

alternative (*adj.*) not traditional; not following the usual options or styles, or accepting something that you can use instead of something else

chiefly (*adv.*) mainly, mostly

compete (*v.*) to try to win or achieve something or to try to be better than someone else

environmentally (*adv.*) related to the natural world (land, sea, air) in which we live

recycling (*n.*) the process used to make objects and materials reusable

release (*v.*) to let substances escape into the air, oceans, and so on

renewable (*adj.*) can be continued or replaced so that it is never finished or used completely

resources (*n.*) things that a person or country has or can use

unique (*adj.*) not like anyone or anything else; being the only one of its type

waste (*n.*) material food that is not needed and is therefore thrown away

---

From:	Daniel Ramirez
To:	Pedro Ramirez
Subject:	Carbon Footprint Meeting

Hi Dad,

I just returned from a city planning meeting about reducing our carbon footprint. It was scary, but also exciting to hear all of the ideas people had. It was scary because I never knew how much carbon dioxide cities produce. Cities are responsible for 70 to 80 percent of the carbon dioxide that activities and products _____ into the air. In addition, our cities produce
(1)
so much _____! We don't think about how much garbage we
(2)
throw out or how much water we use.

The speakers at the meeting said that _____ is very

(3)

important. We shouldn't throw away materials like newspapers, magazines,

cans, and bottles. They also explained some of the problems with the

traditional sources of energy we use now, especially fossil fuels like oil and

coal. In the 21st century, cities need to explore _____ energy

(4)

sources, like solar and wind power, for heating and transportation. It was

exciting to hear about new buildings that are _____ friendly.

(5)

They are powered _____ by solar and wind power. These

(6)

energy sources are _____. Unlike oil, they will always be

(7)

available, and they leave almost no carbon footprint. It was also exciting to hear

about a new type of streetcar that runs completely on batteries. It would be

_____ to our city to have this type of transportation—no city has

(8)

ever done this before!

I think it's great that companies are now eager to become involved with

these "green" projects. A number of companies will _____

(9)

to be hired to make the changes proposed. Together, city officials,

companies, and environmental experts can combine their knowledge and

_____ to investigate these new ideas and make them a reality.

(10)

I'm glad I went to the meeting. It gave me some ideas on how our city can

make big changes to help keep our world healthy.

Talk to you soon,

Pedro

PREVIEW READING 1

This is an article from a news website. It describes a brand-new city that is being built in Abu Dhabi, one of the emirates that make up the United Arab Emirates.

Read the first and last paragraphs. Check (✓) the kinds of energy you think this new city will use.

☐ oil   ☐ wind   ☐ solar

☐ electricity   ☐ coal   ☐ water

CD 2
Track 12   **Read the article.**

New Zero-Carbon City to Be Built

1   The desert sands of Abu Dhabi seem an unlikely place to build an **environmentally** sound city. A desert is not the first place that comes to mind when you think of "sustainability[1]". In addition, Abu Dhabi, part of the United Arab Emirates, is one of the largest oil producers in the world. But unlikely or not, a new "eco-city" is being built there. Masdar, meaning "the source" in Arabic, will be the first zero-carbon city, meaning the amount of CO_2 **released** into the air will be close to zero.

2   Masdar City will cost $22 billion to build and will use many different forms of energy, including solar and wind. The entire city will be powered by these **renewable** forms of energy. The first part of this project is the construction of one of the largest solar energy plants in the world. This plant will provide most of the energy for the entire city. When Masdar City is completed, it will be six square kilometers in size and will be the home to more than 50,000 people.

artist's rendition of a street scene in Masdar, Abu Dhabi

3   Masdar City will be **unique** not only in its sustainability, but in many other ways. First, there will be no cars within the city's walls. A personal rapid transit (PRT) system will run under the city. A PRT is similar to a car, but runs on magnetic tracks. When you want to travel to another part of the city, you step into your PRT, program it to go to one of the 1,500 stations, and then sit back and relax. Second, **recycling** is central to the development of the city. Even in the construction process, recycled materials will be used. Water will

---

[1] **sustainability:** the ability to continually exist without having a negative effect on the surroundings

be recycled and reused; for example, in the irrigation[2] of crops, any unused water will be used again and again. Human **waste** will be recovered and reused to create soil that can be used in various parts of the city.

4   The city itself will be designed to fit in with its surroundings, with narrow streets and building styles reminiscent of ancient cities in the area. The city is situated so that it gets a great deal of sun on one side, while breezes off the Gulf help to cool it on the other. Additionally, the solar panels atop the buildings will shade the walking areas so that they will remain cool and sheltered from the sun. The entire city will be walled, to prevent noise and dust from entering.

5   Many people and companies around the world have joined the project. The prestigious Massachusetts Institute of Technology will have a branch of its college in the city, the Masdar Institute of Science and Technology (MIST). It will recruit[3] the best students from around the world to do research, **chiefly** in the area of **alternative** energy. Additionally, companies, such as General Electric in the United States and SunTech, a Chinese solar panel manufacturer, have joined to help make Masdar a reality. This has become a truly global project.

Post your comments:

6   **aboutimesue28:** This project sounds awesome! It's just the right combination of factors: the oil-rich country has the money and **resources** to investigate new sources of energy. Countries all over the world have the brains and expertise to help with finding new technology. And companies will **compete** to get involved in this first-ever carbon-emission-free city! Way to go, Masdar!

7   **curioustoknow76:** It's really surprising to me that a country that is one of the world's top oil producers would be building a city like this. But I think it's great! Maybe even the oil-rich countries realize that it will be harder and harder to meet the world's demands for oil, and therefore we need to find new sources of energy.

8   **realitysam:** I have to say to curioustoknow76 that the oil producers want to continue to be very much involved in the energy business. That's the biggest reason why they have decided to invest in renewable energy. They know that the world is slowly coming to believe that we have to change our ways, and they want to be at the forefront of new technology.

9   **annoyed55:** I don't understand why money is being spent on a new city. At a point in time when we all have to make changes in our existing lives, the world focuses on this new high-tech city, which will be home to only 50,000 people! What about the cities that are home to millions? They're falling apart! And they use an incredible amount of energy to function! We have to do something about these cities now. It's very nice to build new cities with new technology, but first we need to focus our attention on existing cities!

10   **Ecogeek66:** In this description of Masdar, it's "almost" zero-carbon. Solar panels don't work at night, so Masdar will have to "borrow" power from other (not green) energy sources during those times. Since Masdar will give back its extra power to the fossil fuel-powered source during daylight, this is considered to be an even trade. And what about the surrounding areas in Abu Dhabi? Just outside Masdar, you will find many carbon-producing plants!

---

[2] **irrigation:** the action of supplying land and crops with water by using pipes, equipment, etc.

[3] **recruit:** to persuade someone to become a member of a school or organization

MAIN IDEAS

Circle the answer that best completes each statement.

1. According to the reading, it's unexpected that Abu Dhabi would build an eco-city because _____.
   a. the weather is beautiful there
   b. it produces a lot of oil
   c. it's such a small place

2. Masdar will be unique because of _____.
   a. its recycling program
   b. its new alternative energy sources
   c. its highways

3. What will be the main focus of study at the new college in Masdar?
   a. the arts
   b. new medical breakthroughs
   c. alternative energy

4. The comments posted after the article _____.
   a. are all favorable
   b. are mixed
   c. are all unfavorable

DETAILS

Reread Reading 1. Then answer the questions.

1. How much will it cost to build Masdar City?

   _____

2. How large will the city be?

   _____

3. How many people will live in Masdar City?

   _____

4. Why will there be no cars in Masdar?

   _____

5. How many PRT stations will there be?

_____

6. Why is SunTech involved in Masdar?

_____

7. Who posted a comment saying that building Masdar is a bad idea?

_____

8. Who posted a comment saying that building Masdar is a business investment more than an environmental one?

_____

 ## WHAT DO YOU THINK?

Discuss the questions in a group. Then choose one question and write five to eight sentences in response.

1. Would you like to live in a city with no cars? Why or why not?

2. Can you think of some advantages to living in a city like Masdar? Can you think of disadvantages?

3. The people who posted comments on the article have different opinions about Masdar. With whom do you agree? Explain.

Reading Skill | **Making inferences**

Making inferences means reading "between the lines" of a text. This means that a reader guesses something is true, based on what is written and on his or her knowledge about the topic. Making inferences is a very useful skill for reading. It's a way to get more information from a text beyond what is written.

Read this sentence from Reading 1.

> A desert is not the first place that comes to mind when you think of "sustainability."

What can you infer from this sentence? What do you think of when you see the word *desert*? It's hot in the desert. There isn't much water. It can be difficult for plants and animals to survive there. You can use what's written and what you already know to infer that it is not usual to think of sustainability in the desert.

A. Read the sentences. Circle the inference that can be made from each statement.

1. As more people move to cities, there is a tremendous strain on public transportation systems.
   a. Trains and buses will need to run more frequently and will probably break down more often.
   b. The systems are old and need to be repaired.

2. If cities are to survive into the 21st century, they need to become more sustainable.
   a. They need to have more hotels and places for people to live; if they don't, cities won't survive.
   b. Cities need to provide more of their own food and energy; if they don't, they won't survive.

3. One way to use less energy is to buy food that is produced locally.
   a. Transporting food requires energy.
   b. Food tastes better when it is grown close to home.

4. If cities are made more "walkable," less energy will be used.
   a. People will lose weight by walking more.
   b. People won't be taking forms of transportation that use fossil fuel if they're walking.

B. Read the sentences about Reading 1. Check (✓) the inferences that can be made from the reading. Find the sentence(s) in Reading 1 that support the answers you checked.

☑ 1. There will be no roads in Masdar.

   First, there will be no cars within the city's walls.

☐ 2. You won't be able to leave the city.

   _____

☐ 3. It's very sunny in Abu Dhabi.

   _____

☐ 4. There will be no oil-powered energy plants in Masdar.

   _____

☐ 5. Students who come to study at MIST are interested in building another city like Masdar.

   _____

READING 2 | "Out of the Box" Ideas for Greener Cities

VOCABULARY

Here are some words and phrases from Reading 2. Read the sentences. Circle the word or phrase that best matches the meaning of each bold word or phrase.

1. Our new heating system is very **efficient**. We were amazed at how well it works and how much money we saved. (expensive / effective / complex)

2. The wind turbines **generate** so much energy that the farm sells some of it back to the electric company. (create / use / lose)

3. Our apartment building has a large vegetable garden on the roof, and we sell the **produce** to the vegetable market in our neighborhood. (meat and fish / fuel and energy / fruits and vegetables)

4. The difference between **urban** residents and country residents is that those living outside of cities are dependent on using cars. (country / city / international)

5. The time has come to think of different ways to farm instead of the **traditional** farming methods. (creative / usual / unusual)

6. Leaving a large carbon footprint now may **threaten** the future of our planet. (risk / help / support)

7. The river that runs through the city has become very **polluted** from all of the garbage and chemicals that have been poured into it. (deep / clean / dirty)

8. Isabel volunteered to help **restore** the old art museum in the city. She helped paint the outside and rebuild the roof. (damage / fix / sell)

9. The new mayor is concentrating on "greening" the city by planting more trees and opening more parks; this is one way to improve the **quality of life** for residents. (well-being / choices / energy)

10. Scientists have been looking for **innovative** ways to produce energy; they know the olds ways won't work forever. (cheap / new / strong)

PREVIEW READING 2

This is a news magazine article called *"Out of the Box" Ideas for Greener Cities*. "Out of the box" means new and different. The article discusses new ways to solve some of the typical problems in cities.

Read the first sentence of each paragraph. Check (✓) the areas you think this magazine article will discuss.

☐ transportation   ☐ crime
☐ heating/cooling systems ☐ pollution
☐ planting/parks/trees   ☐ population

CD 2
Track 13   **Read the article.**

"Out of the Box" Ideas for Greener Cities

1   In attempts to make cities more energy **efficient**, local governments have been putting up solar panels on rooftops and adding wind turbines to the waterfront—both to **generate** energy from "free" sources. These are not new ideas, but they're becoming more and more common and even expected in any plans to make cities greener, or less dependent on energy from coal or oil.

The Urban Farmer

2   But there are some new ideas that may seem a bit strange. How about gathering your homegrown vegetables from your roof? Instead of growing fruits and vegetables in rolling fields, miles away from cities, grow them in the city—on rooftops, in backyards, on vacant lots. A school in New York City has constructed a small farm on part of its playground, and the **produce** is sold during the summer at local farm stands. Across the world, small **urban** farms are "sprouting" up to help make the cities green and to feed urban dwellers.

3   There's even talk of bringing farming inside. A company, Valcent, in El Paso, Texas, is testing indoor farming. The test farm consists of rows of vertical panels filled with potted plants. The whole farm is one-eighth of an acre and is expected to

grow 15 times more lettuce than a **traditional** farm, but use only 5 percent of the amount of water. There are many experiments like this one going on in cities.

the restored Cheonggye Stream in Seoul, South Korea

Build It Up

4   Taking this idea a few steps further, Dickson Despommier, professor of environmental sciences and microbiology at Columbia University, believes that one day skyscrapers will be the farms of the future, providing enough food for entire cities. As he describes the advantages of indoor farming in a recent newspaper article, "You can control nothing

| Reading and Writing   **165**

outdoors, and you can control everything indoors." Crops grown in a controlled environment will not be **threatened** by floods[1], droughts[2], or storms. In addition, the costs will be greatly lowered because no herbicides or pesticides would be used, and the food would not need to be transported great distances.

Tear It Down

5   Another "greening" idea that may seem a little unusual involves transportation within cities. You've heard of building, repairing, and widening roads for the benefit of car travel. Well, what about tearing them down? This is happening in many cities around the world from Paris to Toronto to San Francisco and New York—all in attempts to make the cities greener.

6   In Seoul, South Korea, the Cheonggye Stream runs through the middle of the city. Over the centuries, as the city became more and more crowded, the stream and its many tributaries became very **polluted**. By the 1960s, part of the stream was so polluted that it was decided it would be best to bury it underground. After it was buried, a highway was built over it. This whole construction process took over 30 years.

7   In 2001, the new mayor of Seoul, Lee Myung-bak, promised to **restore** the stream to Seoul because it had become such an eyesore[3], and he wanted to reduce the number of cars in the city. It took four years as the freeway was demolished[4], and much of the concrete recycled. In September 2005, the restored stream was reopened. It now is a park-like area renewing the **quality of life** of downtown Seoul.

Bicing in Barcelona

Keep It Simple

8   Sometimes solutions can be very simple. Take the city of Barcelona, Spain. In 2007, it started a program called "Bicing." At over 400 stations in the city, you can rent one of 6,000 bicycles for up to two hours. The first 30 minutes are free, and you can return the bike to any station. The bike stations are close to other transportation stations, like buses and the metro. Barcelona is very hilly, so many people ride the bikes down the hills and then take public transportation up the hills. Since the program started, the number of stations has increased, and so has the number of subscribers, which in February 2009 was 186,000, or 9 percent of the population. But perhaps the best part of Bicing is that the city's CO_2 emissions decreased by more than 960 tons in the first six months of the program.

9   Cities all over the world have to think of ways to become more energy efficient. Maybe it's time to think "out of the box" for really **innovative** ways to solve this worldwide problem. It will involve changing the way we think of things, but in the end our quality of life will be improved.

---

[1] **flood:** an overflowing of a large amount of water
[2] **drought:** a long period of time with no rain
[3] **eyesore:** something that is unpleasant to look at
[4] **demolish:** to tear something down

MAIN IDEAS

Read the sentences about the article. Write *MI* for main idea and *SD* for supporting detail.

SD 1. A school in New York City made a small farm on part of its playground and sells the produce during the summer.

____ 2. Growing fruits and vegetables in cities is one idea people have for making cities greener.

____ 3. A professor at Columbia University believes that skyscrapers will be farms.

____ 4. Tearing down highways and replacing them with parks is another way to make cities green.

____ 5. Part of a river in South Korea became so polluted that the government decided to bury it.

____ 6. The mayor of Seoul removed a freeway and restored a river.

____ 7. Increasing the use of bicycles for transportation is a simple idea.

____ 8. Barcelona started a bike rental program called Bicing and reduced its CO_2 emissions by 960 tons in the first six months.

DETAILS

Look at the list of advantages of "out of the box" ideas from Reading 2. Write each advantage in the correct column of the chart.

Floods and droughts won't affect crops.	a decrease in CO_2 emissions
fewer cars in the city	no herbicides or pesticides
~~a park-like area~~	quality of life improved
more "green space"	

"OUT OF THE BOX IDEAS"		
Urban Farming	Tearing Down Highways	"Bicing" Program
	a park-like area	

 **WHAT DO YOU THINK?**

A. Discuss the questions in a group.

 **Critical Thinking**

In Activity B, you have to choose among three possible solutions. In doing so, you **conclude** that one way will be better, based on reasons, explanations, and your own knowledge and experience. Making these decisions helps you clarify your own thinking.

1. Which of the ideas mentioned in Reading 2 do you think is the most interesting? Explain.

2. Do you think any of the ideas mentioned in Reading 2 could be used in your town or city? If so, which ones? How do you think they could help improve the quality of life?

B. Think about both Reading 1 and Reading 2 as you discuss the question. Then write five to eight sentences in response.

Both of the readings discuss ways not only to lower carbon emissions, but also to improve quality of life. Which idea do you think will improve the quality of life the most in cities of the 21st century—eliminating the dependence on cars, using renewable energy, or creating more "green space"?

| Vocabulary Skill | Participles as adjectives | |

One way to increase your vocabulary is to learn the different forms of a word. For example, the past participle form of many verbs can be used as an adjective.

             verb

He <u>recycled</u> his old books by donating them to the library.

           adjective

<u>Recycled</u> paper is sent to a company and made into newspaper.

You can guess a word's use by the context and where it is in the sentence. In the first sentence, *recycled* comes after the subject, so you can guess that it is a verb.

In the second sentence, *recycled* is followed by a noun, so you can guess that it is an adjective. Remember that the past participle of a regular verb looks the same as the simple past form.

A. Read each sentence. Write *adjective* or *verb* for each underlined word.

1. The carrots were grown in a <u>controlled</u> environment. _____*adjective*_____

2. They <u>controlled</u> every step of the experiment. _____

3. The <u>increased</u> use of alternative energy has a positive effect on cities.

_____

4. They <u>increased</u> the amount of time they spend walking.

   _____

5. The <u>reduced</u> amount of oil available forces us to rethink our use of

   energy. _____

6. They <u>reduced</u> their dependence on oil by switching to solar energy.

   _____

7. The company <u>polluted</u> the river with the chemicals used in its factory.

   _____

8. The <u>polluted</u> water is harmful to the fish. _____

9. He has <u>worn</u> the same clothes every day for a week. _____

10. They needed gently <u>worn</u> clothes to donate to the children who had lost

    everything in the storm. _____

a clothing donation bin

B. Write sentences using five of the words from Activity A. Be prepared to hand in or share your work.

1. _____

2. _____

3. _____

4. _____

5. _____

WRITING

A **problem/solution essay** describes a problem and gives some suggestions for solving the problem. A good problem/solution essay includes a **thesis statement** that introduces the topic and states what the problem is, two or more body paragraphs that describe possible solutions to the problem, and a concluding paragraph that restates the problem and summarizes the solutions.

The thesis statement gives the main idea of the whole essay. In the introductory paragraph of a problem/solution essay, the thesis statement describes the situation that has caused a problem and states specifically what the problem is. The thesis statement below is underlined.

> Today everyone is very concerned about the environment, in particular global warming caused by CO_2 emissions. <u>Since our cities are responsible for producing most (80 percent) of the world's dangerous carbon emissions, they need to focus on lowering their carbon emissions.</u>

The body of the essay describes possible solutions to the problem stated in the thesis statement. Each body paragraph describes a solution and includes details that explain how or why each solution will work.

Body paragraph 1
Topic sentence
Solution 1
> One way to lower carbon emissions in cities is to use renewable energy sources for heating and cooling buildings.

Body paragraph 2
Topic sentence
Solution 2
> Another way to lower carbon emissions is to develop more efficient public transportation systems.

Body paragraph 3
Topic sentence
Solution 3
> Finally, we need to provide more green space and plant more trees to help absorb the CO_2 emissions.

The concluding paragraph summarizes the problem and the solutions described in the essay.

Tip for Success

Problem/solution essays use phrases such as these for the body paragraphs:

One solution to the problem …

Another way to solve the problem …

An additional solution to the problem …

A. Read the problem/solution essay.

Ideas for Ending Our Traffic Problems

We live in a beautiful city that has so much to offer its residents: museums, theaters, many restaurants, and large parks. But our city also has many problems that need to be addressed. Our downtown area is so congested with traffic at times that it is impossible to get anywhere: Buses can't move, nor can delivery trucks or people trying to walk. The air is filled with exhaust from cars and buses that are unable to move. Currently our downtown area is not a pleasant place to be because of the congestion, and this is a serious situation that needs to be addressed immediately.

First, we need to ban passenger cars from the downtown area. This would allow trucks to make their deliveries more quickly. Also, people would be able to walk the streets without the risk of being killed. The width of the sidewalks could be expanded, allowing for more pedestrian traffic. With fewer vehicles, CO_2 emissions would be lowered, meaning air quality would improve.

Second, if we ban cars from our downtown areas, we will need to provide alternative forms of transportation for people coming to shop and visit. One way to do this is with streetcars. One hundred years ago, when there were fewer cars, the air quality was much better, and people were used to using streetcars to get from place to place. People could leave their cars at home and take a streetcar into the downtown area. Since streetcars are electric, there would be no increase in CO_2 fumes.

Another way to decrease the traffic of our downtown area is to encourage people to ride bikes. This would require building more biking lanes. Bike racks could be built at various locations around the city. Bike rental systems like the ones in Barcelona and Paris would help promote the use of bikes for those who don't own them.

Our downtown area has become extremely crowded in recent years, and it's time to start taking action to change this. Eliminating cars from downtown, introducing a streetcar system, and creating bike lanes are a few possible solutions to improve our city. One result will be an improved downtown area. Another result will be increased profits for downtown businesses.

B. Answer these questions about the essay in Activity A.

1. What is the thesis statement in the introductory paragraph? Underline it.

2. What is the first solution that the writer suggests to solve the problem in body paragraph 1? Put brackets around this information with the number 1.

3. What is the second solution that the writer suggests to solve the problem in body paragraph 2? Put brackets around this information with the number 2.

4. What is the third solution that the writer suggests to solve this problem in body paragraph 3? Put brackets around this paragraph with the number 3.

5. Does the concluding paragraph summarize the problem and solutions described in the essay? Underline the sentence that summarizes the problem. Circle the sentence that summarizes the solutions.

6. Do you agree with the writer's suggested solutions? Why or why not?

Grammar Passive voice

The **passive voice** changes the word order of a sentence in the **active voice**. In a sentence in the active voice, the *subject* comes before the *object*. In a sentence with the passive voice, the *object* becomes the *subject*.

> Farmers **sell** their produce at local farm stands. (active)
> Produce **is sold** at local farm stands by farmers. (passive)

In sentences with the active voice, the *agent* (doer of the action) is the subject. In passive voice sentences, the *object* (noun receiving the action) is the subject.

>   agent   receiver
> Tanya **made** the coffee. (active)
>
>   receiver   agent
> The coffee **was made** by Tanya. (passive)

Use the passive voice when you want to focus on the receiver of the action. Use the active voice when you want to focus on the agent or doer of the action.

The passive voice is formed by *be* + **past participle** (*by* + **noun**).

> The entire city **is powered** by renewable forms of energy.
> A highway **was built** over the river.
> Cars **will be eliminated** from city centers.

 for Success

The passive voice is often used in news reporting.

A. Look at Reading 2. Find three examples of sentences with the passive voice. Write them on the lines.

1. _____

_____

2. _____

_____

3. _____

_____

B. Rewrite the sentences. Use the passive voice.

1. They constructed a beautiful garden on top of the apartment building.

   A beautiful garden was constructed on top of the apartment building.

2. They planted a vegetable farm in a 20-story skyscraper.

   _____

3. Solar panels produced the energy for construction of the city.

   _____

4. They tore down the entire highway in 12 months.

   _____

5. They built a beautiful park in the area that was once an eyesore.

   _____

People in a city can enjoy green space.

In this assignment, you are going to write a problem/solution essay in which you describe how your city can become a better place to live. You could also write about your home, school, or neighborhood. As you prepare your essay, think about the Unit Question, "How can we make our cities better places to live?" Refer to the Self-Assessment checklist on page 176. Use information from Readings 1 and 2 and your work in this unit to support your ideas.

For alternative unit assignments, see the *Q: Skills for Success Teacher's Handbook.*

PLAN AND WRITE

A. BRAINSTORM Think of a problem in your city, home, school, or neighborhood. Write it in your notebook. Then brainstorm a list of possible solutions to the problem.

B. PLAN Look at your list of possible solutions from Activity A. Circle your best ideas. Then write an outline for your essay.

1. **Introductory paragraph:** Write a thesis statement that describes the situation that caused the problem and states specifically what the problem is.

_____

_____

_____

_____

2. **Body paragraph 1:** Describe one suggestion for solving this problem.

_____

_____

_____

Give details that explain how or why the solution will work.

_____

_____

_____

3. **Body paragraph 2:** Describe a second suggestion for solving this problem.

_____

_____

_____

Give details that explain how or why the solution will work.

_____

_____

_____

4. **Body paragraph 3:** (optional) Describe a third suggestion for solving this problem.

_____

_____

_____

Give details that explain how or why the solution will work.

_____

_____

_____

5. **Concluding paragraph:** Summarize the problem and the suggested solutions.

_____

_____

_____

_____

C. **WRITE** Write your essay in your notebook. Use your outline from Activity B. Include the problem and at least two solutions to the problem. Write four to five paragraphs. Look at the Self-Assessment checklist on page 176 to guide your writing.

REVISE AND EDIT

A. PEER REVIEW Read a partner's essay. Answer the questions and discuss your answers with your partner.

1. Is the problem clearly described in the introductory paragraph?

2. Does the thesis statement state the problem? Underline it.

3. Are there at least two solutions to how the problem can be solved in two body paragraphs?

4. Is there a summary of the problem and solutions in the concluding paragraph?

B. REWRITE Review the answers to the questions in Activity A. You may want to revise and rewrite your essay.

C. EDIT Complete the Self-Assessment checklist as you prepare to write the final draft of your essay. Be prepared to hand in your work or discuss it in class.

SELF-ASSESSMENT		
Yes	**No**	
☐	☐	Is the punctuation correct?
☐	☐	Are all words spelled correctly?
☐	☐	Does the essay include vocabulary from the unit?
☐	☐	Does the essay begin with an introductory paragraph that contains a thesis statement?
☐	☐	Does the thesis statement describe the situation that caused the problem and specifically state what the problem is?
☐	☐	Does the essay include two or three body paragraphs that suggest solutions?
☐	☐	Does the essay include a concluding paragraph that summarizes the problem and suggests solutions?
☐	☐	Is the passive voice used correctly?
☐	☐	Are participles used as adjectives? If so, are they formed correctly?

Track Your Success

Circle the words you learned in this unit.

Nouns
produce
recycling
resource AWL ⚷
waste ⚷

Verbs
compete ⚷
generate AWL ⚷
release AWL ⚷
restore AWL ⚷
threaten ⚷

Adjectives
alternative AWL ⚷
efficient ⚷
innovative AWL
polluted
renewable
traditional ⚷ AWL
unique ⚷ AWL
urban ⚷
worn

Adverbs
chiefly
environmentally AWL

Phrase
quality of life

⚷ Oxford 3000™ words
AWL Academic Word List

Check (✓) the skills you learned. If you need more work on a skill, refer to the page(s) in parentheses.

READING	●	I can make inferences. (p. 162)
VOCABULARY	●	I can use participles as adjectives. (p. 168)
WRITING	●	I can write a problem/solution essay with a thesis statement. (p. 170)
GRAMMAR	●	I can use the passive voice. (p. 172)
LEARNING OUTCOME	●	I can write a problem/solution essay describing how my city can become a better place to live.

READING	●	using a timeline
VOCABULARY	●	collocations with nouns
WRITING	●	writing a cause/effect essay
GRAMMAR	●	complex sentences to show cause and effect

Unit QUESTION

How can a small amount of money make a big difference?

PREVIEW THE UNIT

A Discuss these questions with your classmates.

Have you ever given money to help someone or an organization? How did it make you feel?

What kinds of organizations typically ask for money? How is the money used?

Look at the photo. What do you think is happening?

B Discuss the Unit Question above with your classmates.

Listen to *The Q Classroom*, Track 2 on CD 3, to hear other answers.

179

C The pictures show things that don't cost a lot of money, but they can have very positive results. What do you think these results might be? Match the pictures with the results.

A | a goat

B | a honeybee

C | a lamb

D | chicks

E | silkworms

F | school supplies

___ education   ___ honey   ___ silk

___ eggs   ___ milk   ___ wool

D Read the saying. Then discuss the questions with a partner.

> Give a man a fish, and you feed him for a day. Teach a man to fish, and you feed him for a lifetime.

What do you think this saying means? How do you think the things in Activity C might relate to the saying?

VOCABULARY

Here are some words from Reading 1. Read the sentences. Then write each bold word next to the correct definition.

1. Maya's parents were very **proud** of her for graduating with honors.

2. John is graduating from college soon. Yesterday he said, "I **owe** it all to my parents. Without their support, I couldn't have done it."

3. Mr. Buffett, the man who donated the money, is **extremely** rich and enjoys sharing his wealth.

4. Because of her good grades and leadership activities, Gabriella was able to **attend** the college she wanted.

5. When I arrived in the United States, my cousin provided me with a home, food, and money until I was able to find a job. I'm very grateful for her **generosity**.

6. When his parents agreed to pay for his education, Juan made a **commitment** to them that he would finish college.

7. The relief organization is collecting food and supplies, which it will **distribute** to victims of the earthquake.

8. When Carl meets his sister's students, it might **inspire** him to become a teacher, too.

9. Getting a part-time job at college is a good way to prepare yourself for the **transition** from school to the workforce.

10. Moving to England was a big **adjustment** for Fatima. She had to learn English and get used to cold weather.

a. _____ (*n.*) a state of getting used to new conditions or a new situation

b. _____ (*v.*) to go to or be present at a place

c. _____ (*n.*) something you have promised to do; a responsibility

d. _____ (*v.*) to give things to a number of people

e. _____ (*adv.*) very

f. _____ (*n.*) the quality of giving more help or money than is usual or necessary

g. _____ (*v.*) to give a feeling of wanting and being able to do something good

h. _____ (*v.*) to exist or be successful because of someone or something

i. _____ (*adj.*) pleased and satisfied because you or someone you are close to has done something good

j. _____ (*n.*) a change from one condition or form to another

volunteers unpacking supplies

PREVIEW READING 1

You are going to read an article from a news magazine. The article tells the story of a girl from a very poor village in Uganda who became a college graduate with the help of people who donated money to an organization.

Read the first and last paragraphs. What kind of help do you think this girl received? Check (✓) your answers.

☐ money
☐ clothing
☐ food
☐ a tutor
☐ books
☐ an animal

How a Ugandan Girl Got an Education

1   Among the **proud** students receiving diplomas[1] at the 2008 graduation ceremony at Connecticut College was a young woman from Uganda named Beatrice Biira. And what makes her accomplishment so special is that she **owes** it all to a goat.

2   Beatrice grew up in the village of Kisinga in the mountains of Uganda. It is an **extremely** poor village, and Beatrice, the second oldest of six children, wanted very much to **attend** school, but her family didn't have the money to pay for it. In fact, the family was so poor that there was often not enough to eat. The only clothing Beatrice owned was a red dress that was cut open in the back so that she could grow into it.

3   All of this changed in 1993, when Beatrice was 9 years old, and her mother told her that, through the **generosity** of an organization named Heifer,

they had received a goat. A goat? At the time, Beatrice could not see the value of something like a goat, especially when her mother told her that she would be responsible for caring for the goat.

4   Heifer International is a charity based in Little Rock, Arkansas which raises money to send animals to people in very poor countries. Its goal is to help people to become self-sufficient[2] by providing them with the animals and the education needed to care for them. The people receiving their help have to make the **commitment** to pass the gift on to others. Beatrice's mother and others in her village had applied to Heifer to receive help. The help came in the form of 12 goats that were **distributed** to the people in their village. Beatrice's family received one of these goats.

5   They named the goat Mugisa, which in Lokonzo, Beatrice's language, means "luck." And soon Beatrice realized how her luck would change because of this goat. Mugisa was pregnant when she came to Beatrice's family and soon gave birth to two more goats. The milk from the goats helped Beatrice and her siblings to get healthier, and they were soon able to sell the additional milk. The family earned enough money to send Beatrice to school.

6   Though Beatrice was much older than the other children in school, she didn't mind. She breezed through the early grades as an excellent student. One day in 1995 a study tour, sponsored

---

[1] **diploma:** the official piece of paper that shows you have completed a course of study

[2] **self-sufficient:** able to produce everything that you need without help from or having to buy from others

by Heifer, came to visit Beatrice's village. Two women who accompanied the tour, Page McBrier and Lori Lohstoeter, were impressed by Beatrice's passion for learning. They were **inspired** by her story and decided to write a children's book about her. They called it *Beatrice's Goat*.

7   Beatrice continued to be an excellent student and won a scholarship[3] to a high school in Kampala, the capital of Uganda. While Beatrice was a student there in 2001, *Beatrice's Goat* was published and became a very popular *New York Times* bestseller. Beatrice was asked by Heifer to go on a book tour to the United States. While on this trip, she met a woman, Rosalee Sinn, who would become a great help to her. Ms. Sinn and others helped her obtain a full scholarship to attend the Northfield Mount Hermon School in Massachusetts, a private preparatory school that had a program to help international students make the **transition** to college. For Beatrice, perhaps the biggest **adjustment** was the weather. She had never experienced cold weather before.

8   Despite the adjustments, Beatrice did very well at Northfield Mount Hermon, and while she was there, she applied to 11 colleges. She was accepted to half a dozen colleges, including some very prestigious ones. She decided to go to Connecticut College, where she won a scholarship. At first she wanted to become a veterinarian, but she soon decided to study economics and international studies. She wants to return to Uganda one day and use what she has learned to help her countrymen.

9   So in June 2008, there stood Beatrice in her cap and gown. This once very poor little girl from one of the poorest villages in the world was now a college graduate—all because of a goat!

---

[3] **scholarship:** money that is given to a person by an organization or a school to help pay for his/her studies

MAIN IDEAS

Read the sentences. Write the correct paragraph number next to each main idea.

_____ 1.   Beatrice grew up in Uganda in a very poor family.

_____ 2.   Heifer International helps people by giving them animals and teaching them how to care for them.

_____ 3.   Beatrice's studies continued as she received scholarships to high school and a preparatory school.

_____ 4.   Her mother contacted Heifer, and life changed for Beatrice and her family.

_____ 5.   As a result of receiving a goat, Beatrice's family had enough money to send her to school.

DETAILS

Read the statements. Write *T* (true) or *F* (false). Then correct each false statement to make it true.

____ 1.   Beatrice was happy when she learned about receiving a goat.

____ 2.   Beatrice's mother had applied to an organization to get help.

____ 3.   Beatrice's family soon had three goats.

____ 4.   Beatrice had trouble learning in school because she was so much younger than the other children.

____ 5.   Two women met Beatrice and decided to write a book about her, called *Beatrice's Story*.

____ 6.   The biggest adjustment to studying in the United States for Beatrice was the food.

____ 7.   She received a scholarship to go to a college in Connecticut.

____ 8.   She graduated from college in 2008.

 WHAT DO YOU THINK?

Discuss the questions in a group. Then choose one question and write five to eight sentences in response.

1.   Some good things happened after Beatrice's family received the goat: the goat produced milk, which helped make the family healthier, and the family sold the extra milk for money. What were some other benefits?

2.   What qualities do you think Beatrice has that have helped her be successful in her goals?

3.   Have you, or has someone you know, ever received a small amount of help that had big, positive results? Explain.

A **timeline** shows all of the important events that happened during a period of time. Timelines can be useful for understanding and remembering the events in a reading text. Look at the timeline for Reading 1, "How a Ugandan Girl Got an Education."

Beatrice's Life

1984	Beatrice was born.
1993	A goat was donated to Beatrice's family.
1995	A study tour sponsored by Heifer came to Beatrice's village.
2001	The book *Beatrice's Goat* was published.
2008	Beatrice graduated from Connecticut College.

 **for Success**

A timeline is useful when reading a text in which many events occur. You can make a timeline as you're reading the text and then refer to it later.

A. Read the article. Then complete the timeline on page 187.

From Salad Dressing to Summer Camp

Did you know that spending a few dollars on a bottle of salad dressing could help children with serious illnesses enjoy a week at summer camp? It's true, thanks to Newman's Own.

In December 1980, Paul Newman, a famous American film actor, and his friend A. E. Hotchner made gallons of salad dressing to give to family and friends as gifts. Their friends loved it and wanted more, so Hotchner and Newman made more. But this time they decided to sell the rest, and Newman's Own was born.

By the end of 1982, the first year of production, profits were close to $400,000. Since neither Newman nor Hotchner needed money, Newman said, "Let's give it all away to those who need it." Over the years, Newman's Own added more and more products. By the end of 2008, more than 40 products were being sold, and all of the profits went to charity, more than $265 million worth as of April 2009.

The profits have been donated to various charities, but the one closest to Newman's heart was the Hole in the Wall Gang camp, founded in 1988. This special camp is for seriously ill children. For one week, children at this camp can forget about their illnesses and enjoy themselves. Medical needs are taken care of, and since they are all sick, the children don't have to feel "different." It's all paid for through people buying salad dressing—a small price for such a great reward.

The Hole in the Wall Gang camp is founded.

Newman and Hotchner bottle salad dressing for gifts.

More than 40 Newman's Own products are sold.

Profits are close to $400,000.

History of Newman's Own

1980 _____

1982 _____

1988 _____

2008 _____

READING 2 | Money Makes You Happy—If You Spend It on Others

VOCABULARY

Here are some words and phrases from Reading 2. Read the sentences. Circle the answer that best matches the meaning of each bold word or phrase.

1. The new business had many **positive** results for the family: it increased their income and brought them pride and satisfaction.

    a. financial

    b. unwanted

    c. good

2. We were very surprised by the results of the study. We didn't **suspect** that the person with less money would be happier.

    a. hope

    b. guess

    c. discover

3. It is good to keep a record of your test scores so that you can **measure** your progress throughout the semester.

    a. judge the amount of

    b. think about

    c. invent

4. My son is very **selfish** with his toys. He needs to learn to share with other children.
   a. thinking only of yourself
   b. thinking of others
   c. intelligent

5. Graduating from college was a **remarkable** achievement for Beatrice since she wasn't able to attend school until she was nine years old.
   a. unusual
   b. average
   c. frustrating

6. Researchers have found that people **tend to** be happier when they are doing things to benefit others.
   a. decide to
   b. want to
   c. are likely to

7. People say money can't buy happiness, and studies have shown that after people win the lottery their happiness can actually **decrease**.
   a. go up
   b. go down
   c. remain the same

8. Participating in class and talking to your teacher can **enhance** your learning experience.
   a. improve
   b. ruin
   c. continue

9. We chose Ms. Chang to manage the project because she's very **reliable**. Everyone trusts her.
   a. hard
   b. dependable
   c. favorable

This is an article from a news website. It discusses the results of research done on the relationship between money and happiness.

Read the first sentence of each paragraph. What do you think the article will say? Check (✓) your answer.

- ☐ The more money you give away, the happier you will be.
- ☐ Giving away a small amount of money makes you happier than spending it on yourself.

 CD 3
Track 4 **Read the article.**

Money Makes You Happy— If You Spend It on Others

1   They say money can't buy you happiness, but new research published in the journal *Science* suggests that it can, if you spend it on someone else. "Simply making very small changes in how you spend money can make a difference for happiness," said Elizabeth Dunn, an assistant professor at the University of British Columbia, who led the research along with Michael I. Norton, an assistant professor at Harvard Business School. Studies of happiness have long found that, unless people are extremely poor, getting more money brings surprisingly small gains in **positive** feelings. The researchers **suspected** that perhaps the reason people weren't happier was not because of the money itself, but rather because of what they did with their money—mainly, spending it on possessions for themselves.

2   The research was done at a small Boston-area medical supply company, where employees received bonuses[1] averaging about $5,000. The researchers **measured** their levels of happiness before and after receiving the money. What they found, said Norton, was that "the size of the bonus you get has no relation to how happy you are, but the amount you spend on other people does predict how happy you are."

3   The researchers used a five-point scale, asking people, "Do you feel happy in general?" There were five answers provided: yes, most of the time, sometimes, rarely, or no. They found that people could expect to go up a full point on the scale if they spent about a third of the bonus on others, Dunn said. She calls this "prosocial" spending. She continued with the example of Tim and Dan: They both answered the question that they were happy "sometimes" before receiving the bonus. If Dan spent a third of his bonus "prosocially" and Tim spent none in this way, the researchers would expect that after spending their bonuses, Dan would be happy "most of the time." This is exactly what happened.

4   The study fits in well with other current research that finds that helping others is the best way to help yourself. People who give more and are more socially connected are happier. "There's

---

[1] **bonuses:** payments that are added to what is the usual amount of pay/salary

so much benefit to the person who contributes to others that I often think that there is no more **selfish** act than a generous act," said Tal Ben-Shahar, author of the book *Happier* and teacher of a positive psychology course on happiness, Harvard's most popular class. During one week of the course, Ben-Shahar asks students to do five small acts of kindness a day. Examples of these could be giving change to homeless people, being nice to waiters, or calling grandparents. "The effect of it is quite **remarkable** and lasts for much longer than a day," he said.

5   Similarly, the *Science* study found that spending a small amount of money could bring large results. In a separate experiment, the researchers gave college students either $5 or $20 and told them to quickly spend the money. Some were told to spend it on themselves—on a bill or a gift to themselves. And some were told to spend it on others—on a donation to charity, or a gift to someone else. The vast majority of the students predicted that they would be happier with $20 than $5.

6   That evening, the participants' happiness levels were measured. But again, the amount of money did not matter. Those who spent it on others felt happier than those who spent it on themselves. "We don't want to suggest that more money would never matter," Dunn said. "It's just that in our studies we found that how people spent their money mattered at least as much as how much money they received.

Indeed, there was no effect at all on the amount of money received [in the two studies]."

7   Part of the explanation could be that people **tend to** be made happier by experiences than by possessions, said Sonja Lyubomirsky, author of *The How of Happiness*. Americans tend to spend their money on possessions, she said, but research shows that the happiness from a bigger house or television set quickly **decreases** as people get used to the benefits and face the responsibility that comes with ownership. However, taking a friend out to lunch, say, is more of an experience and more likely to bring longer-lasting good feelings. Also, when a person acts kindly, she said, "There are social consequences: You might **enhance** your friendship. You might make new friends. People might reciprocate[2]."

8   So why don't more people realize that spending money on others is a **reliable** road to happiness? One reason may be because it's much easier to count money than to measure happiness, Norton said. "If you think about getting ahead in life, you can say, 'Last year I made X, and now I'm making X plus 10.' But people don't conceive of their lives as 'I was 71 happy last year, and now I'm 76 happy.'" Even if they do, the reasons for greater happiness may not be obvious to them, he said.

9   Dunn said that when she wrote up the study, it was close to the holidays, and she decided that, instead of giving her family things, she would get them gift certificates to a website that allows people to choose various philanthropic[3] projects to support. "I've never gotten more positive responses to any gift I've given my family," she said. "I was giving them the gift of giving."

[2] **reciprocate:** to behave or feel toward someone in the same way as he/she behaves or feels towards you

[3] **philanthropic:** helping the poor and those in need, especially by giving money

MAIN IDEAS

Circle the answer that best completes each statement.

1. The research discussed in the reading dealt with money and its effect on people's ____.
   a. happiness
   b. health
   c. generosity

2. Researchers found that people were happier if they spent part of their bonus on ____.
   a. things/possessions for themselves
   b. others
   c. things/possessions for their families

3. Professor Tal Ben-Shahar asks students to do five small acts of kindness each day for a week. The effect of this on the students is ____.
   a. positive
   b. negative
   c. neutral

4. In one experiment, students were given a small amount of money to spend on others or on themselves, and the results showed that those who spent it on others were ____.
   a. happier
   b. slightly less happy
   c. wealthier

5. One reason for the results of the experiment is that when people spend money on others, ____.
   a. the effect lasts longer than when they spend on themselves
   b. they don't regret it
   c. they don't waste money

DETAILS

Match each question with the correct answer.

_____ 1. What did the research in *Science* show?

_____ 2. How did the researchers measure the employees' happiness?

_____ 3. How did the first study fit in with other recent research?

_____ 4. What did Professor Tal Ben-Shahar discover?

_____ 5. What was the result of research involving college students who were given $5 or $20 to spend?

_____ 6. What possible explanation is given for the results of the studies led by Dunn and Norton?

a. People are happier from experiences than from possessions.

b. The effect of giving lasted longer than expected.

c. It showed that small changes in spending affect happiness.

d. It showed that you help yourself when you help others.

e. The amount of money did not affect students' happiness.

f. They used a five-point scale.

 WHAT DO YOU THINK?

A. Discuss the questions in a group. Then choose one question and write five to eight sentences in response.

1. Have you ever given a small amount of money to someone? If so, how did it make you feel? If not, are there other "acts of kindness" that you have done? How did you feel afterwards?

2. Have you ever bought something because you thought it would make you happy, only to find that the happiness didn't last long? If so, what happened?

B. Think about both Reading 1 and Reading 2 as you discuss the question.

Both readings are about giving a small amount of money to others. The effect of this giving is positive for both the giver and the receiver. Who do you think benefits more? Why?

One way to improve your vocabulary is to learn new **collocations**. As you learned in Unit 3, collocations are words that are frequently used together. Learning collocations can help your writing sound more natural. Look at these examples of collocations from the readings.

> <u>Through the generosity</u> of an organization named Heifer, Beatrice's family received a goat.
>
> During one week of the course, Ben-Shahar asks students to do five small <u>acts of kindness</u> a day.

Read the list of collocations that use the nouns *generosity* and *kindness*.

through the generosity of (someone): because of the donations (money) or kindness of (someone)
extraordinary generosity: the quality of being willing to give, or the act of giving an unusual amount of time or money
generosity toward (someone): unselfish actions that help someone

an act of kindness: a small action to help someone
treat (someone) with kindness: to behave in a compassionate way toward someone
the kindness of strangers: help from people you don't know

A. Read the paragraph. Underline the collocations from the Vocabulary Skill box.

Unexpected Help

In May 2008, a very strong tornado raced through a small town in the plains of Kansas. As a result, the home of the Milano family was completely destroyed. They lost everything they owned. But a remarkable thing happened after the storm passed. The town came together and showed <u>extraordinary generosity</u>. Someone offered them a place to live. Many families came to offer food, clothing, and things like blankets and pillows. The Milanos were treated with kindness by their neighbors. Through the generosity of a wealthy businessman, the Milanos had enough money to begin to rebuild their home. Mrs. Milano was amazed at the kindness of strangers; people she had never met sent checks and clothing from miles away. But perhaps the biggest act of generosity came from a young girl who gave her bicycle to the youngest Milano child.

B. Choose three collocations from the Skill Box. Write a sentence using each collocation in your notebook.

Writing Skill Writing a cause/effect essay

A **cause/effect** essay analyzes the causes (reasons) and effects (results) of a situation or event. A cause/effect essay includes an introductory paragraph, body paragraphs, and a concluding paragraph.

In a cause/effect essay, the **introductory paragraph** describes the situation or cause, gives background information, and includes a thesis statement (main idea). The thesis statement in a cause/effect essay describes the effects of the situation.

The **body paragraphs** of an essay provide support for the thesis statement. In a cause/effect essay, each body paragraph includes a topic sentence that states a supporting point and describes an effect. Other sentences in a body paragraph provide examples, details, or facts.

In a cause/effect essay, the **concluding paragraph** restates the main idea and often offers some additional thoughts or predictions for the future.

A. Read the cause/effect essay. Underline the thesis statement.

My Friend Bill

In one of my college classes this semester, we were required to do an act of kindness for the elderly. My project involved buying food and preparing lunch for an elderly person. I spent about $10. The lunch included soup, a sandwich, and dessert. I packed up the lunch and went off to meet my new friend. A project like this one can result in new friendships, less loneliness, and the possible discovery of a career path!

The person I visited was an 85-year-old man named Bill, who was unable to walk more than a few steps due to health issues. When I brought him the meal, he was very happy to see me. He has no family, and the only person he sees is the nurse's aide who comes every morning to help him get dressed and to give him his medicine. It was a treat for him to eat a meal with someone because he usually eats alone. He thought the food was great, but even more than the food, he enjoyed having someone to talk to.

When I started talking to Bill, I found out that he had had a very interesting life. He had been a train engineer when train travel was much more popular. He had so many interesting stories to tell about his travels and adventures while working on the railroad. I really enjoyed talking to him, and it was especially interesting to me because I was planning a trip over the summer to see other parts of the country. I had been considering traveling by train, and after meeting Bill, I have no doubt in my mind that I will be going by train.

Perhaps the biggest effect of this project was that I realized that working with the elderly is an area that I'm very interested in. I found out that I enjoy spending time

with older people; they have so much life experience to offer. I am a good listener, and older people sometimes just want someone to listen to them, so it seems like a perfect match. As a result, I plan on focusing my studies on the elderly.

What started out as just another assignment for my class resulted in much more than I expected. It's hard to know who was affected more by this project, Bill or me. I learned how easy it is to be a great help to someone else. The reward that I received was in knowing I had helped someone; but I also met a person whom I truly enjoyed talking to and spending time with. I plan to continue to bring lunch to Bill once a week, but it won't be as part of my class work. It will be because I genuinely enjoy his company, and I think he enjoys mine as well. Hopefully in the future, I will be able to work with the elderly so that I can help even more people like Bill.

B. Complete the graphic organizer with information from the essay in Activity A.

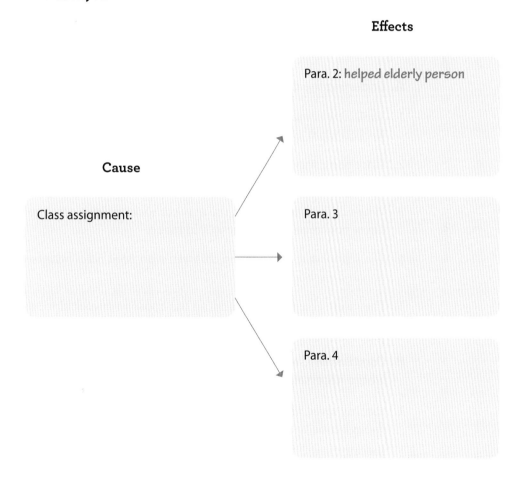

Effects

Para. 2: *helped elderly person*

Cause

Class assignment:

Para. 3

Para. 4

for Success

Dependent clauses with *because*, *since*, and *when* are frequently used in cause/effect essays. The dependent clause with *because*, *since*, or *when* is the "cause" and the main clause is the "effect."

A **complex sentence** has an independent clause, or main clause, and one or more dependent clauses. A **clause** is a group of words that has a subject and a verb. An independent clause can stand alone as a complete sentence. A dependent clause cannot stand alone and must be used with a main clause. Dependent clauses that show **cause** can begin with subordinators like *because*, *since*, and *when*. Look at these examples.

Beatrice was not very happy **when** her mother told her about the goat.

Because people in the United States donated money, her family received a goat.

The parts of the sentences beginning with *because*, *since*, and *when* are dependent clauses. If a dependent clause comes before the main clause, it is followed by a comma.

dependent clause	main clause
Because people in the United States donated money,	her family received a goat.

A. Underline the dependent clauses.

1. Their new computer repair business grew in the first year <u>because they all worked night and day</u>.

2. Since there was very little rain all spring, the amount of corn grown was very small.

3. When he invested $300 in the new company many years ago, he didn't know how much money he would make.

4. The school can now pick up children who need rides because someone donated a school bus.

5. They were able to finish building the house in a week since many volunteers came to help.

B. Combine the sentences with the words in parentheses. Use a comma where necessary.

1. Sammy saved all of the money he made in his summer job. He finally had enough money to buy a car.

   (because)

   Because Sammy saved all of the money he made in his summer job, he finally

   had enough money to buy a car.

2. The village no longer floods. The villagers planted a hundred trees on the hillside.

   (since)

   _____

   _____

3. The organization had received enough donations. It bought the new equipment.

   (when)

   _____

   _____

4. Mr. Kelly donated a great deal of money to the children's fund. He knew that the children needed a new school.

   (because)

   _____

   _____

5. People in the village suffered from extreme poverty. Many families could not afford to send their children to school.

   (since)

   _____

   _____

Unit Assignment | Write a cause/effect essay

 In this assignment, you are going to write a five-paragraph cause/effect essay. As you prepare your essay, think about the Unit Question, "How can a small amount of money or a simple act of kindness make a big difference?" Refer to the Self-Assessment checklist on page 200. Use information from Readings 1 and 2 and your work in this unit to support your ideas.

For alternative unit assignments, see the *Q: Skills for Success Teacher's Handbook*.

PLAN AND WRITE

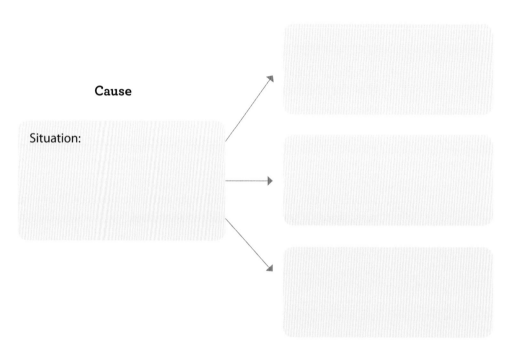

Tip Critical Thinking

The Brainstorm activity asks you to **participate** with your group. When you participate, you work with others to apply what you have learned to a new situation or problem. Active **participation** helps you remember information better.

A. BRAINSTORM Work in a group. Brainstorm situations in which a small amount of money or a simple act of kindness can make a big difference. Write the situations in your notebook.

B. PLAN Follow these steps to plan your essay.

1. Choose one of the situations from Activity A. Think of at least three effects or results of this situation. Complete the graphic organizer with your ideas.

Effects

Cause

Situation:

2. Use your ideas from the graphic organizer to write an outline for your essay.

   A. **Introductory paragraph:** Describe the situation (cause).

   _____

   _____

   Write the background information.

   _____

   _____

   Write your thesis statement describing the effects of the situation.

   _____

   _____

B. **Body paragraph 1:** Write a topic sentence that states a supporting point and describes an effect.

_____

_____

Give examples, details, or facts.

_____

_____

C. **Body paragraph 2:** Write a topic sentence that states a second supporting point and describes an effect.

_____

_____

Give examples, details, or facts.

_____

_____

D. **Body paragraph 3:** Write a topic sentence that states a third supporting point and describes an effect.

_____

_____

Give examples, details, or facts.

_____

_____

E. **Concluding paragraph:** Restate the main idea and offer additional thoughts or predictions for the future.

_____

_____

_____

_____

C. **WRITE** Write a cause/effect essay in your notebook. Use your outline from Activity B. Include at least three effects related to the cause. When appropriate, use _because_, _since_, and _when_. Look at the Self-Assessment checklist on page 200 to guide your writing.

REVISE AND EDIT

A. **PEER REVIEW** Read a partner's essay. Answer the questions and discuss them with your partner.

1. Is the situation clearly described in the introductory paragraph?

2. Does the thesis statement describe the effects of the situation? Underline the thesis statement.

3. Are there at least three results (effects) given in the body paragraphs?

4. Does the concluding paragraph restate the main idea and offer additional thoughts or predictions?

B. **REWRITE** Review the answers to the questions in Activity A. You may want to revise and rewrite your essay.

C. **EDIT** Complete the Self-Assessment checklist as you prepare to write the final draft of your essay. Be prepared to hand in your work or discuss it in class.

	SELF-ASSESSMENT	
Yes	**No**	
☐	☐	Is the punctuation correct?
☐	☐	Are all words spelled correctly?
☐	☐	Does the essay include vocabulary from the unit?
☐	☐	Does the introductory paragraph contain a thesis statement?
☐	☐	Does the introductory paragraph describe the situation (cause) and its effects?
☐	☐	Does the essay include three body paragraphs that each describe an effect?
☐	☐	Does the essay include a concluding paragraph that summarizes the situation (cause) and its effects?
☐	☐	Does the essay include complex sentences? If not, where could one or two be added?
☐	☐	Does the essay include the use of collocations with nouns? If not, where could one or two be added?

Circle the words you learned in this unit.

Nouns
adjustment AWL
commitment 🔑 AWL
generosity
kindness 🔑
transition AWL 🔑

Verbs
attend 🔑
decrease 🔑
distribute AWL 🔑
enhance AWL
inspire 🔑
measure 🔑
owe 🔑
suspect 🔑
tend (to) 🔑

Adjectives
positive AWL 🔑
proud 🔑
reliable AWL
remarkable 🔑
selfish

Adverbs
extremely 🔑

Collocations
an act of kindness
extraordinary generosity
generosity toward
the kindness of strangers
through the generosity
  of (someone)
treat (someone) with
  kindness

🔑 Oxford 3000™ words
AWL Academic Word List

Check (✓) the skills you learned. If you need more work on a skill, refer to the page(s) in parentheses.

READING ⚪	I can use a time line. (p. 186)
VOCABULARY ⚪	I can use collocations with nouns. (p. 193)
GRAMMAR ⚪	I can write a cause/effect essay. (p. 194)
WRITING ⚪	I can use complex sentences. (p. 196)
LEARNING OUTCOME ⚫	I can write a cause/effect essay explaining how a small amount of money can make a big difference.

READING	●	identifying the author's purpose, audience, and tone
VOCABULARY	●	using the dictionary
WRITING	●	writing an opinion essay with a counterargument
GRAMMAR	●	sentence fragments

LEARNING OUTCOME

Develop an essay about communication that states your personal opinion and gives a counterargument.

Unit QUESTION

Do people communicate better now than in the past?

PREVIEW THE UNIT

A Discuss these questions with your classmates.

How do you usually communicate with your family and friends?

Do you use social networking sites on the computer? Why or why not?

Look at the photo. Why do you think the woman is using two phones?

B Discuss the Unit Question above with your classmates.

Listen to *The Q Classroom*, Track 5 on CD 3, to hear other answers.

C Look at the abbreviations from text messages. Check (✓) the ones you know. Write out their meanings. Then compare your answers with a partner.

✓ a. lol   _laughing out loud_

___ b. brb   _____

___ c. btw   _____

___ d. ttyl   _____

___ e. g2g   _____

___ f. gr8   _____

___ g. jk   _____

D What situations do you think are appropriate for texting? Complete the survey. Then discuss your answers with a partner.

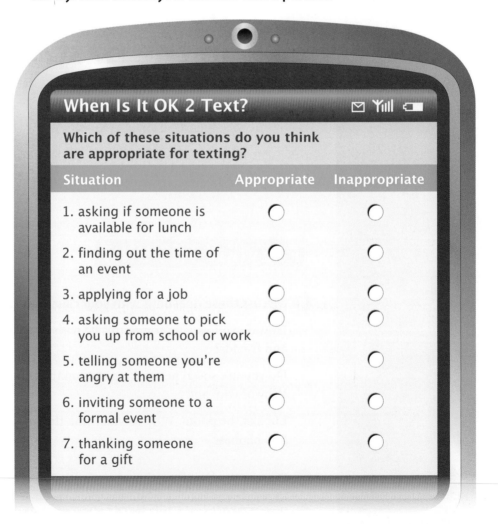

When Is It OK 2 Text?

Which of these situations do you think are appropriate for texting?

Situation	Appropriate	Inappropriate
1. asking if someone is available for lunch	○	○
2. finding out the time of an event	○	○
3. applying for a job	○	○
4. asking someone to pick you up from school or work	○	○
5. telling someone you're angry at them	○	○
6. inviting someone to a formal event	○	○
7. thanking someone for a gift	○	○

READING

READING 1 | 2b or not 2b?

VOCABULARY

Here are some words from Reading 1. Read the sentences. Circle the answer that best matches the meaning of each bold word.

1. **Curiosity** sometimes leads parents to read their children's emails. They are interested in what they are talking about.
   a. love   b. desire to know   c. shyness

2. Membership in the student council is **restricted** to students who have good grades.
   a. prohibited   b. limited   c. encouraged

3. Email has added a new **dimension** to communication. Today, people can send messages, pictures, and documents almost instantly.
   a. disadvantage   b. result   c. aspect

4. Many teenagers do not use **conventional** spelling when they text their friends. They mix numbers and abbreviations from certain words.
   a. typical   b. unusual   c. foreign

5. One **feature** of many cell phones is a built-in camera.
   a. characteristic   b. gift   c. idea

6. There is **consistency** in her choice of friends. All of her friends are intelligent and interested in technology.
   a. aggressiveness   b. likeness   c. reality

7. We are looking for **creative** employees with new, interesting ideas to help design our website.
   a. imaginative   b. punctual   c. caring

8. Cell phone companies keep improving their products to satisfy the **demands** of their customers.
   a. schedules   b. needs   c. friends

This is a newspaper article. It discusses fears about texting. Look at the title of the article. Written out it would read, "To Be or Not to Be." It is a famous line in *Hamlet*, a play by William Shakespeare. The author uses this title to get readers to think about texting, whether it should exist now, and whether it will exist in the future.

Read the first paragraph. Do you think texting is going to remain a popular form of communication? Why or why not?

CD 3
Track 6   Read the article.

2b or not 2b?

1   As a new variety of language, texting has been condemned[1] as *textese*, *slanguage*, a *digital virus*. Ever since the arrival of printing, people have been arguing that new technology would have disastrous consequences for language. People were worried about the introduction of the telegraph, telephone, and broadcasting. But has there ever been a linguistic phenomenon that has caused such **curiosity**, suspicion, fear, excitement, and enthusiasm all at once as texting—and in such a short space of time? Less than a decade ago, hardly anyone had heard of it.

2   People think that the written language seen on cell phone screens is new and alien[2], but all the popular beliefs about texting are wrong. Its graphic distinctiveness is not a new phenomenon, nor is its use **restricted** to the young. Texting has added a new **dimension** to language use, but its long-term effect is minor. It is not a disaster.

3   Although many texters enjoy breaking linguistic rules, they also know they need to be understood. There is no point in paying to send a message if it breaks so many rules that it is not intelligible. Many texters change just the grammatical words (such as *you* and *be*). Also, **conventional** spelling and punctuation is always used when institutions send out information messages, as in this university text to students: "Weather Alert! No classes today due to snowstorm."

4   There are several distinctive **features** of the way texts are written that combine to give the impression of novelty[3], but none of them is, in fact, linguistically novel. Many of them were being used in chat room communication before the arrival of cell phones. Some can be found in precomputer informal writing, dating back a hundred years or more.

5   The most noticeable feature is the use of single letters, numerals, and symbols to represent words or parts of words, as with *b* (*be*) and *2* (*to*). They are called rebuses, and they go back centuries. Adults who condemn a "c u" in a young person's texting have forgotten that they once did the same thing themselves (though not on a cell phone).

---

[1] **condemn:** to say strongly that something or someone is bad or wrong
[2] **alien:** strange or different

[3] **novelty:** the quality of being new, different, and unusual

6   Similarly, the use of initial letters for whole words, such as *n* for *no*, … and *cmb* for *call me back*, is not at all new. People have been initializing common phrases for ages. *IOU* (I owe you) has been known from the year 1618. There is no difference, apart from the form of communication, between a modern kid's *lol* (laughing out loud) and an earlier generation's *asap* (as soon as possible).

7   In texts we find such forms as *msg* (message) and *xlnt* (excellent). Almst any wrd cn be abbrvted in ths wy—though there is no **consistency** between texters. But this isn't new either. English has had abbreviated words ever since it began to be written down. Words such as *exam*, *vet*, *fridge*, and *bus* are so familiar that they have effectively become new words.

8   What novelty there is in texting lies chiefly in the way it takes some of the processes used in the past one step further. One characteristic runs through all these examples: The letters, symbols, and words are run together, without spaces (*cul8r* = See you later). This is certainly unusual in the history of special writing systems.

9   Texters use deviant spellings—and they know they are deviant. But they are by no means the first to use such nonstandard forms as *cos* (because) or *wot* (what). These are so much a part of English literary tradition that they have been given entries in the *Oxford English Dictionary*. *Cos* is there from 1828 and *wot* from 1829.

10   The need to save time and energy is by no means the whole story of texting. Children quickly learn that one of the most enjoyable things you can do with language is to play with its sounds, words, grammar—and spelling. The desire to be playful is there when we text, and it is hugely powerful. Within two or three years of the arrival of texting, it developed a playful dimension. In short, it's fun.

11   An extraordinary number of prophecies[4] have been made about the linguistic evils unleashed by texting. But five years of research (from a team at Coventry University in the U.K.) has shown that, on the contrary, literacy improves. Researchers have found strong positive links between the use of text language and the skills that are needed for success in standard English in preteenage children. The children who were better at spelling and writing used the most texting.

12   Some people dislike texting. But it is only the latest example of the human ability to be linguistically **creative** and to change language to meet the **demands** of different situations. There is no disaster approaching. We will not see a new generation of adults growing up unable to write proper English. The language as a whole will not decline. In texting what we are seeing, in a small way, is language in evolution.

---

[4] **prophecies:** predictions about the future

MAIN IDEAS

Read the statements. Write *T* (true) or *F* (false). Then correct each false statement to make it true.

____ 1. Many people have condemned texting because they think it will have a bad effect on language.

____ 2. The type of language used in texting is new.

____ 3. Texters may use the language differently, but their messages are still understood.

____ 4. The only new feature of texting is the strange spellings of words.

____ 5. People have a strong desire to be playful, and texting is fun.

____ 6. Research shows that texting improves literacy.

____ 7. Texting is an example of how language evolves.

DETAILS

Read the sentences. Order the details from 1 to 6 according to when they occur in the article.

____ a. Some features of the way texts are written date back 100 years or more.

____ b. IOU (I owe you) dates from the year 1618.

____ c. Researchers found that children who were better at spelling and writing used the most texting.

____ d. People were worried that the telegraph, telephone, and broadcasting would change language.

____ e. Single letters, numerals, and symbols used to represent words or parts of words are called rebuses.

____ f. Many texters change only grammatical words (such as *see*) in their messages.

WHAT DO YOU THINK?

Discuss the questions in a group. Then choose one question and write five to eight sentences in response.

1. Do you think texting has changed language? If so, do you think this is a good thing or a bad thing? Explain.

2. The author says that texting is an example of how creative humans can be with language. Do you agree or disagree with this statement? Why?

3. What do you think are the advantages of texting? What do you think the disadvantages are?

Reading Skill | **Identifying the author's purpose, audience, and tone**

Writers have a **purpose** for their writing. For example, a writer may want to *explain*, *inform*, *describe*, *persuade*, *entertain*, or *give an opinion* of something. Sometimes a writer has more than one purpose.

Writers use words in ways that create different **tones**, or moods, in their work. For example, a written passage can have a serious, light and playful, or funny tone. The tone of the writing depends on the **audience**, the people reading the piece, and is determined by the words the writer chooses. The tone tells us how the author feels about the subject.

A. **Look back at Reading 1. Answer these questions in your notebook.**

1. Who is the audience for this piece? How do you know this?

2. What is the author's purpose for writing this article? What sentence in the reading tells you this? Underline it.

3. How can you describe the writer's tone? Find examples in the reading to support your ideas. Put a check mark (✓) next to them.

It's useful to identify an author's tone and purpose when you read. You should also keep your purpose and audience in mind when you write and use the appropriate tone.

B. Read each excerpt. Choose the writer's purpose and tone from the boxes. Remember, a writer may have more than one purpose.

Purpose		Tone
to describe something	to express an opinion	funny
to entertain the reader	to inform the reader	light and playful
to explain something	to persuade the reader	serious

1. A trip to the city of Charleston, South Carolina, is an enjoyable experience. Not only is the weather perfect, but the ambiance of the old-fashioned streets brings you back to a simpler time. There are a few spots that cannot be missed on your visit.

   Purpose: _____

   Tone: _____

2. Installing a new television is not as simple as it used to be, but if you follow these steps, it should take only an hour or so.

   Purpose: _____

   Tone: _____

3. The number of accidents involving teenage drivers is enormous. Last year alone, 70 percent of fatal accidents involved teen drivers. It is time to raise the driving age to 20 for these and many other reasons.

   Purpose: _____

   Tone: _____

4. I thought I knew a lot about being a parent until I became one. It really is not that difficult; that is, if you don't mind having spaghetti poured on your head or having grape juice spilled all over your brand-new white pants. Oh, and then there's the part about sleeping, or *not* sleeping, as the case may be with parenting.

   Purpose: _____

   Tone: _____

| # Social Networking Sites: Are They Changing Human Communication?

VOCABULARY

Here are some words from Reading 2. Read their definitions. Then complete each sentence.

> **complementary** (*adj.*) going well together; adding something that the other thing does not have
>
> **debatable** (*adj.*) not certain; something that could be argued about
>
> **instantaneous** (*adj.*) happening at once or immediately
>
> **moderation** (*n.*) the quality of being able to control your actions so that they are within sensible limits
>
> **potentially** (*adv.*) possibly
>
> **react** (*v.*) to behave in a certain way because of what someone says or does
>
> **reconsider** (*v.*) to think again about something
>
> **shorten** (*v.*) to become not as long or to make something become not as long
>
> **warn** (*v.*) to tell someone to be careful or aware of something, often bad, that exists or might happen

1. The issue of texting is still _____. People disagree about whether the effects of texting are positive or negative.

2. I was planning to get my 12-year-old daughter a cell phone, but now I'm not sure if it's a good idea. I might _____ my decision.

3. Parents should _____ children that communicating with strangers on the Internet can be dangerous.

4. People _____ differently to changes in technology. Some people are excited to learn about new devices, while others feel safer using what they already know.

5. Spending too much time on the Internet could _____ cause someone to be less social in real life.

6. Jeanne planned to take a five-day vacation, but she had to _____ it because of an urgent meeting at work.

7. I like paying bills online because it is _____. As soon as I click the "pay" button, the payment is made.

8. She believes in _____. She never eats too much or works too hard.

9. We make a good team because our skills are different, but _____. I love talking to clients, and Leila is great at managing our finances.

PREVIEW READING 2

This is a magazine article. It discusses the results of research done on social networking sites. Social networking sites are websites that allow people to share information, pictures, music, and interests with others.

Read the first sentence of each paragraph. What do researchers say about social networking sites? Check (✓) your answer(s).

☐ Social networking sites are bad for people.
☐ Social networking sites might be dangerous.
☐ Social networking sites are good for people.

 CD 3 Track 7 **Read the article.**

Social Networking Sites: Are They Changing Human Communication?

1 It is hardly news that people are using the Internet for communicating with others more and more. Internet use comes in various forms, from email to IMs to social networking sites, like Facebook, MySpace, or Bebo. Some people fear that someday we will no longer feel the need to talk to one another face-to-face. However, some recent studies suggest that people communicate, or stay in touch, even *more* than they used to. Whichever side you fall on, what is clear and not **debatable**, is that human communication has changed in the 21st century. But results of recent scientific studies may have us **reconsider** just how much our new communication forms have changed our world.

2 In June 2008 a British psychiatrist, Himanshu Tyagi, **warned** that communicating on social networking sites could have a negative effect on the generation of people born after 1990. This generation has never known a world without the Internet. Tyagi says that these people use the Internet to communicate with others so much that

they may have trouble forming real relationships. Tyagi is concerned that people can start and end relationships over the Internet. As he described the Internet, "It's a world where everything moves fast and changes all the time, where relationships are quickly disposed of at the click of a mouse."

3   Another psychologist, Dr. Aric Sigman, warned of physical effects of using social networking sites. He suggests that the decrease in the amount of time we spend interacting with people face-to-face could have biological effects on the human body. The results of his study suggest that, without real personal interaction, the body does not **react** the same way it would if people were meeting face-to-face. As a result, immune responses, even hormone levels can be changed. These changes can **potentially** lead to the development of illnesses, such as cancer.

4   Finally, another British scientist, Susan Greenfield, warned members of the British government that social networking sites could actually be changing the human mind, making it more childlike. She fears that attention spans have been **shortened** because of so much time spent in front of screens where everything is **instantaneous**. Since everything, including responses, is immediate on social networking sites, in actual life people may expect an immediate response; when this doesn't happen, their behavior can be described as almost childlike.

5   Despite all of these warnings, studies can be found that demonstrate the positive aspects of social networking sites. The results of one study show that using social networking sites has boosted the self-esteem of young adults. Another suggests that college students using these sites feel more "connected" with people when they use them. In addition to scientific studies, there are many who feel that the benefits of social networking sites far outweigh the possible negative aspects. Many people, especially those who spend a lot of time at home, for various reasons, find the Internet a lifeline[1]. They are able to communicate with many people using these sites.

6   Perhaps the key to this new communication style is **moderation** and common sense. If someone spends all of his time on the Internet, and never actually sees friends face-to-face, that seems like an unhealthy way to live. But if someone spends time on the Internet, some of which is spent arranging meetings for "real" time together, then it seems almost **complementary**. Moderation is the key to keeping communication alive and well in the 21st century.

[1] **lifeline:** something a person needs in order to survive a difficult situation

MAIN IDEAS

Read the sentences. Then number them in the order that the ideas appear in Reading 2.

_____ a. Using social networking sites could affect the human mind and behavior.

_____ b. There may be negative effects on the human body without real personal interaction.

_____ c. According to some studies and many people, social networking sites have benefits.

_____ d. The key to communicating on the Internet may be moderation and common sense.

_____ e. People are increasingly using the Internet for communication with others.

_____ f. Communicating on social networking sites could have a negative effect on people born after 1990.

DETAILS

Complete each sentence with a word or phrase from the box.

a lifeline	self-esteem
a social networking site	the development of illnesses
real relationships with people	

1. Facebook is an example of _____.

2. Himanshu Tyagi warned that those born after 1990 may have trouble forming _____.

3. Dr. Aric Sigman believes that without real personal interaction, biological changes in the body may lead to _____.

4. In one study with a group of young adults using social networking sites, there was an increase in _____.

5. Many people who spend a lot of time at home find the Internet

_____.

 **WHAT DO YOU THINK?**

A. Discuss the questions in a group. Then choose one question and write five to eight sentences in response.

1. What do you think is the main reason that people use social networking sites?

2. Do you think any of the warnings mentioned in the article are anything to be concerned about? Why? Why not?

3. The conclusion the author reaches is that using these sites and meeting someone in person can be complementary. Do you agree with this?

B. Think about both Reading 1 and Reading 2 as you discuss the question.

Has communication improved or been harmed as a result of texting and social networking sites? Explain.

| Vocabulary Skill | Using the dictionary | |

A **prefix** is a group of letters at the beginning of some words that can help you guess a word's meaning. Some prefixes change the meaning of the base word to its opposite. Look at this example from the readings.

… that seems like an <u>unhealthy</u> way to live. (**Un**healthy means "not healthy.")

Here are some other prefixes that mean *no* or *not*.

a-	*Atypical* means "not typical."
dis-	*Disconnected* means "not connected."
im-	*Impossible* means "not possible."
non-	*Nonstop* means "does not stop."

Here are some other common prefixes.

bi-	two
con-	with; together
de-	taking away; the opposite
in-	(**il-, im-, ir-**) not
inter-	between; among
out-	beyond; out of the usual
pre-	before
re-	again
self-	relating to oneself; by one's own efforts

You can use a dictionary to find the meanings of other prefixes.

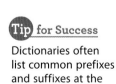 **Tip for Success**

Dictionaries often list common prefixes and suffixes at the back of the book.

A. Match each word from Reading 1 with its definition.

_____ 1. informal (Paragraph 4)

_____ 2. precomputer (Paragraph 4)

_____ 3. unusual (Paragraph 8)

_____ 4. nonstandard (Paragraph 9)

_____ 5. preteenage (Paragraph 11)

_____ 6. unleashed (Paragraph 11)

_____ 7. dislike (Paragraph 12)

_____ 8. unable (Paragraph 12)

a. not considered correct

b. not of the form accepted as standard

c. to think something or someone is not pleasant

d. suitable for a friendly situation

e. to let a strong force, etc. be felt or have an effect

f. not having the time, knowledge, or skill to do something

g. before computers were used

h. under the age of thirteen

B. Look at these words from Reading 2. Try to guess their meanings. Then match each word with its definition. Check your answers in the dictionary.

_____ 1. **inter**action

_____ 2. **out**weigh

_____ 3. **re**consider

_____ 4. **self**-esteem

a. to be more important than something else

b. a feeling of being happy with oneself

c. to think again about something

d. the act of working together or mixing

C. Choose five words from Activity A and Activity B. Write a sentence using each word.

_____

_____

_____

_____

_____

| Writing Skill | Writing an opinion essay with a counterargument | |

Like an opinion paragraph, an **opinion essay** expresses how you feel about a topic. For example, it might express whether you agree or disagree with an idea.

The **introductory paragraph** in an opinion essay includes the thesis statement, which clearly states the writer's opinion or view of something. In the introductory paragraph of an opinion essay, the writer states an opinion about the topic. The introductory paragraph may include background information and a **counterargument** to the writer's opinion. A counterargument is the opposite opinion. Writers sometimes mention a counterargument and then explain why it's not true in order to make their point stronger.

Each **body paragraph** of an opinion essay includes a topic sentence that states a reason for the writer's opinion. Examples or facts are given to support each reason.

The **concluding paragraph** of an opinion essay restates the opinion and refers to the counterargument. A concluding paragraph also summarizes the reasons the writer has this opinion. Often, the concluding paragraph includes an additional idea, sometimes a prediction, about the topic.

 **for Success**

Writers use certain phrases to introduce a counterargument, such as these:
Some people say that …
Some people think that …
Some people argue that …

A. Read the opinion essay.

In Praise of Technology

Communication in the 21st century has changed a lot. Now it's so easy to talk to people because of computers and cell phones. Some people think that we communicate less frequently because talking is becoming a thing of the past, whether in person or on the phone. I don't think that is the case. In fact, I think it's just the opposite. Just because we don't "talk" on the phone as much as we used to doesn't mean that we communicate less frequently. We just prefer typing, whether it's a text message on a cell phone, an email, or an instant message on the computer. This type of messaging is preferable to talking on the phone because it's fast, convenient, and fun.

First, you have to type in your message or note, and this is actually faster than using a phone. If you call someone, you may not reach the person, so you leave a message. The person may not call back when you're free, so he or she leaves a message, and you begin playing "phone tag." If you email or text your friend, you simply have to wait until he or she responds.

Second, it's very convenient. It's particularly convenient for places like schools. Say you're a parent, and you need to contact your child's teacher. Most teachers don't have access to phones during the day, so it's difficult to reach them. If you leave them an email, they can check when they have a break or at lunch and respond to the email.

Sara Mannion uses email to contact her older children at school. "Children are not allowed to use cell phones during the school day, but sometimes I need to remind one of my children about something important. Rather than have the school secretary find my child in a class to give him the message, I leave a text message on his phone. So at the end of school, he'll have the reminder that he has a dentist appointment," says Mannion.

Finally, using email can be a fun way to stay in touch with people you don't see that often or who live far away. Jack Bianco started a reunion of his elementary school friends a few years ago. "I could never have gotten in touch with all of my friends without the Internet and emailing. It's great. I've 'spoken' with people whom I haven't seen in years. It's great catching up this way. I wouldn't have been able to do it by calling all of these people." Besides reunions, people use emailing for clubs, athletic teams, and organizations in which all of the members can be reached by one simple email.

We now have new technology that some people think is making talking and using the phone go out of style. But text messaging and emails are just an easier way to communicate with people. Though we may not talk on the phone as often as we did 50 years ago, it's still important for most of us to hear the voice of people we care about. It just may be preceded by a text or email saying, "Let me know when you're free to talk."

B. Reread the essay in Activity A. Then answer the questions.

1. Look at the introductory paragraph. Which sentence describes the writer's opinion about the topic? Underline it. What is the counterargument? Draw a circle around it.

2. Look at the body paragraphs. What are the three reasons that the writer gives for his or her opinion?

   Reason 1: _____

   _____

   Reason 2: _____

   _____

   Reason 3: _____

   _____

3. Look at the concluding paragraph. Does the writer add another idea to the essay? If so, what is it?

   _____

   _____

A **sentence fragment** is an incomplete sentence that cannot stand alone. Sentence fragments are usually considered errors. It is important to avoid sentence fragments in your writing. Look at the examples.

> **Fragment:** When you write a text message.
>
> **Fragment:** Because I like to text my friends late at night.

As you learned in Unit 9, these examples are dependent clauses. When used alone, they are fragments. They need to be combined with a main clause.

> <u>When you write a text message</u>, you don't have to spell every word correctly.
>
> I go to sleep very late <u>because I like to text my friends late at night</u>.

Words such as *because*, *since*, *although*, *when*, or *after* are often used with dependent clauses. These words connect an incomplete sentence to a main clause to avoid a fragment.

A. Read the sentences. Identify each sentence as a complete sentence (S) or a sentence fragment (F). Correct the sentence fragments with a partner.

_____ 1. When I can't talk to someone on the phone.

_____ 2. He likes to text his friends late at night because it doesn't disturb anyone in the house.

_____ 3. After I finish all of my homework.

_____ 4. I stay in touch with all of my friends when I go on Facebook.

_____ 5. Although she's a very sociable person.

B. Read the paragraph and correct any fragments.

> I love going on social networking sites. When I was in high school. I was a very shy person. It was difficult for me to speak with people. Because I was so shy. Then someone invited me to be his friend on Bebo. I signed up, and two more people invited me to be their friends. Soon, I had many friends. We talked about lots of things, like school and sports. Although I saw these people in school every day. There was something about talking to them on Bebo that seemed different. Now I have more friends than I ever had. Because I'm not shy on the computer.

Tip **Critical Thinking**

In the Unit Assignment, you are asked to write an opinion essay with a counter argument. In effect, you are **defending** your opinion by using your reasons and arguing against the other side's reasons. **Defending** your ideas makes you think about them more deeply.

In this assignment, you are going to write a five-paragraph essay describing your opinion about whether communication in the 21st century has changed for the better or for the worse. As you prepare your essay, think about the Unit Question, "Do people communicate better now than in the past?" Refer to the Self-Assessment checklist on page 222. Use information from Readings 1 and 2 and your work in this unit to support your ideas.

For alternative unit assignments, see the *Q: Skills for Success Teacher's Handbook.*

PLAN AND WRITE

A. **BRAINSTORM** Follow these steps to help you gather ideas for your essay.

1. In your notebook, brainstorm a list of ways we communicate in the 21st century.

2. In your notebook, brainstorm another list of ways people communicated 50 years ago.

B. **PLAN** Follow these steps to plan your essay.

1. Compare the two lists you wrote in Activity A to help you decide whether communication has improved or not.

2. Write an outline for your essay.

   A. **Introductory paragraph:** State your opinion about the question.

   _____

   _____

   Write the background information. Briefly describe a counterargument.

   _____

   _____

   B. **Body paragraph 1:** Write a topic sentence that states a reason for your opinion.

   _____

   _____

Give examples or facts.

_____

_____

_____

C. **Body paragraph 2:** Write a topic sentence that states a second reason for your opinion.

_____

_____

Give examples or facts.

_____

_____

_____

D. **Body paragraph 3:** Write a topic sentence that states a third reason for your opinion.

_____

_____

Give examples or facts.

_____

_____

_____

E. **Concluding paragraph:** Restate your opinion, refer to your counterargument, and summarize your three reasons.

_____

_____

_____

C. **WRITE** Write your essay in your notebook. Use your outline from Activity B. Include an introductory paragraph with an opinion and counterargument, three paragraphs describing three different reasons for your opinion, and a concluding paragraph restating your opinion and counterargument and summarizing your reasons. Look at the Self-Assessment checklist on page 222 to guide your writing.

REVISE AND EDIT

A. PEER REVIEW Read a partner's essay. Answer the questions and discuss them with your partner.

1. Is a clear opinion expressed in the essay?

2. Does the introductory paragraph clearly state the opinion?

3. Is there a counterargument in the introductory paragraph? Underline it.

4. Are there three body paragraphs that each describe a reason for the opinion? Is each reason supported by examples or facts?

5. Does the concluding paragraph restate the opinion and summarize the reasons?

6. Do you have any suggestions to help improve the organization of the essay?

B. REWRITE Review the answers to the questions in Activity A. You may want to revise and rewrite your essay.

C. EDIT Complete the Self-Assessment checklist as you prepare to write the final draft of your essay. Be prepared to hand in your work or discuss it in class.

SELF-ASSESSMENT		
Yes	No	
☐	☐	Is the punctuation correct?
☐	☐	Are all words spelled correctly?
☐	☐	Does the essay include vocabulary from the unit?
☐	☐	Does the essay include an introductory paragraph that states an opinion and describes a counterargument?
☐	☐	Does the essay include three body paragraphs that each provide reasons and examples or facts?
☐	☐	Does the essay contain a concluding paragraph that restates the opinion and summarizes the reasons?
☐	☐	Are any words with prefixes used correctly?
☐	☐	Are there any sentence fragments? Underline them and then correct them.
☐	☐	Is the tone of the writing appropriate for the audience?

Circle the words you learned in this unit.

Nouns
consistency AWL
curiosity
demand 🔑
dimension AWL
feature AWL 🔑
moderation

Verbs
react 🔑 AWL
reconsider
shorten
warn 🔑

Adjectives
complementary AWL
conventional AWL 🔑
creative AWL 🔑
debatable AWL
instantaneous
restricted 🔑 AWL

Adverb
potentially AWL 🔑

🔑 Oxford 3000™ words
AWL Academic Word List

Check (✓) the skills you learned. If you need more work on a skill, refer to the page(s) in parentheses.

READING	I can identify the author's purpose, audience, and tone. (p. 209)
VOCABULARY	I can use prefixes. (p. 215)
WRITING	I can write an opinion essay with a counterargument. (p. 217)
GRAMMAR	I can recognize and avoid sentence fragments. (p. 219)
LEARNING OUTCOME	I can develop an essay about communication that states my personal opinion and gives a counterargument.